D0951063

Aug 16

UPROOT

UPROOT

TRAVELS IN TWENTY-FIRST-CENTURY
MUSIC AND DIGITAL CULTURE

JACE CLAYTON

FARRAR, STRAUS AND GIROUX   NEW YORK

Farrar, Straus and Giroux
18 West 18th Street, New York 10011

Palm tree image courtesy of iStock.com / Ivan-96.

Library of Congress Cataloging-in-Publication Data
Names: Clayton, Jace, author.
Title: Uproot : travels in twenty-first-century music and digital
    culture / Jace Clayton.
Description: First edition. | New York : Farrar, Straus and Giroux, [2016]
Identifiers: LCCN 2016001906 | ISBN 9780374533427 (pbk.) |
    ISBN 9780374708849 (Ebook)
Subjects: LCSH: Popular music—Social aspects. | Dissemination of music. |
    Music and the internet. | Popular music—Production and direction. |
    FL Studio (Computer file) | Electronic dance music—History and
    criticism. | Popular music—21st century—History and criticism. | Popular
    culture—21st century.
Classification: LCC ML3918.P67 C63 2016 | DDC 781.6409/05—dc23
LC record available at http://lccn.loc.gov/2016001906

Designed by Jo Anne Metsch

Our books may be purchased in bulk for promotional, educational, or
business use. Please contact your local bookseller or the Macmillan Corporate
and Premium Sales Department at 1-800-221-7945, extension 5442,
or by e-mail at MacmillanSpecialMarkets@macmillan.com.

www.fsgbooks.com • www.fsgoriginals.com
www.twitter.com/fsgbooks • www.facebook.com/fsgbooks

1 3 5 7 9 10 8 6 4 2

FOR ROCÍO

We continue to think we are hearing something beautiful, and so we are. Our ears, our hearts, forgive. Music could even be defined by what we happen to be forgiving at a particular time in history.

—ANITA SULLIVAN, *The Seventh Dragon*

Some times the nite is the shape of a ear only it aint a ear we know the shape of. Lissening back for all the souns whatre gone from us . . . Lissening for whats coming as wel.

—RUSSELL HOBAN, *Riddley Walker*

CONTENTS

AUTHOR'S NOTE

For samples of the music referenced in *Uproot* and links to explore further, visit uprootbook.com.

UPROOT

1

CONFESSIONS OF A DJ

The early twenty-first century will be remembered as a time of great forgetting. As so many of our ways of communicating with each other and experiencing the world translate to the digital and dematerialize, much is lost, and many new possibilities emerge. When people look back a hundred years from now, this time will be seen as a crucial turning point, when we went from analog to digital. Much of what is special about this transition gets articulated by music, those waves of magic that happen when the human spirit joins with technology to create vibrations that enchant us regardless of language or age, afloat between novelty and tradition and always asking to be shared.

Zeitgeist heartbeats. A three-minute pop song can stop time, as sure as a three-second sample can conjure up decades of history. Music clocks the speed of our age—then runs it down or winds it up or makes it funky as the moment requires.

In the last twenty years digital technology has without question changed all aspects of music: inspiration, production, distribution, performance, reception—everything. Some of this has been for the bad, but plenty has been for the good. And these profound electronic transformations are only part of the picture. When I reflect on my life since I started DJing internationally in 2000, my head starts to spin. Who knows how many cities and time zones I've passed through. My wife sometimes calls me "the jet-lag king." I've taken easily a thousand flights, and in each destination I've been surprised by on-the-ground details that complicate or outright contradict the standard media narratives about how music is changing. The more I traveled the more I saw how the ways in which we make, access, and value music have shifted, creating new social meanings that get at the heart of what it means to be alive in our wired and unpredictable time.

I've DJed in more than three dozen countries. What I do isn't precisely popular in any of them, but enough people knew me and my music, and were happy to show me what mattered in their scene and why.

It's hard to reach North Cyprus—the top slice of a tiny island in the Mediterranean that seceded after a war with Greece in 1974—not least because only one country, Turkey, officially recognizes it. Yet there we were, whizzing through arid country past pastel bunker-mansions, the architectural embodiment of militarized paranoia and extreme wealth, en route to an empty four-star hotel. We were going to rest for a day and then play music in the ruins of a crusader castle. It was the year 2000. I was the turntablist for an acid jazz group from New York City. The band didn't really need a DJ, but it did need someone to signify "hip-hop," and that was me. There were six of us, including our saxophonist leader, a bassist, a drummer, a Haitian sampler-player, and a singer, Norah Jones, before she was known for anything besides being Ravi Shankar's daughter.

When the cab dropped us off at the hotel, it was practically vacant: four liveried attendants were in the hotel casino, bored behind the empty gaming tables, and a grand total of two other paying guests—elderly British pensioners, holdovers from remembered pre-1974 days when Cyprus was undivided. I unloaded my gear and sat beside the pool, making small talk with our host, trying to figure out exactly why our band had been imported all the way from New York to play an opulent deserted island. Down the coast, thirty miles away in the haze, a tall cluster of glass-and-steel buildings hugged the shore. "What's that city?" I asked. It looked like Miami. "Varosha," she said. Completely evacuated in the 1974 conflict. A ghost town on the dividing line between North and South Cyprus. The only people there were UN patrol units and kids from either side who illegally entered the prohibited zone to live out a J. G. Ballard fantasy of decadent parties in abandoned seaside resorts.

If North Cyprus represented the forgotten side of a fault

line of global conflict, how were we getting paid? Who owned those scattered mansions that we saw on the way from the airport? Was our trip bankrolled with narco-dollars, to please the criminals hiding out in an empty landscape, or with Turkish state funding, to win tourists back? I never found out. I played the show, bought a laptop with my earnings, quit the band, and moved from New York to Madrid.

A few years earlier, I had been living in Cambridge, Massachusetts, attending college while trying to teach myself how to be a DJ. Friends and I began throwing events in nontraditional club spaces—an architect's studio, a cafeteria, the Boston Children's Museum. We were actively mixing things up against the segregationist logic of Boston's dance scene, doing such things as inviting dancehall reggae DJs to perform alongside experimental guitar bands and stocking a room with "noise toys" for audience members to participate in lo-fi electronics jam sessions. It was a fun, heady time. We were starting to draw regular crowds, and gradually I was getting competent on the decks (though I shudder to recall the spectacular mistakes I subjected everyone to in those first few years when my ideas outpaced my technical abilities by a long shot). I was able to develop my style precisely because our little scene was born from frustrations with the standard club experience: we wanted an exploratory, open space.

As I look back on those Boston days, I'm proud of our unspoken belief that if a supportive network came first, exciting musical moments would follow. Journalists love to crown royalty; magazine covers and website banners practically demand it. Yet as I've traveled, time and time again I've found myself in places where musical innovation and excitement emerge from a community experience, wherein the most groundbreaking or influential artists are rarely the most lauded.

In 2001 I recorded a three-turntable, sixty-minute mix called *Gold Teeth Thief*. It was deliberately all over the place: I opened with R&B futurist Missy Elliott and ended with Muslimgauze, an obscure one-man band from Manchester who layered field recordings from the Middle East over trancelike electronic beats. I uploaded the mix to the Internet so my friends could listen. Who else would? One magazine reviewed it, then another, and soon a lot of magazines, leading to hundreds of thousands of downloads. Meanwhile, I had moved to Madrid, happily going about my days without regular Internet access. I didn't know what was up. A few months after the mix went online, I got a phone call from a large European independent label. I'd used one of their songs on the mix. They loved it! It was the best DJ session they'd heard in ages! They wanted to license the *Gold Teeth Thief* mix and give it a proper release, assuming they could pay the various labels a fee of $1,000 per track. "That'd be fantastic," I said, "but pretty expensive. I use forty-four different songs on it. Some of those are major pop tunes, and a bunch are unlicensable bootlegs. It'd be a nightmare to do legally." They insisted that I send a complete track list so that their legal department could get cracking. Result: "Impossible. Our lawyers laughed at us."

As a process, DJing is inevitable and necessary for our times, an elegant way to deal with data overload. As a performance, it's what the kids are grooving to the world over. As a product, it's largely illegal. If I were a band, and *Gold Teeth Thief* an album, not a mix, that would have been my big break. A powerful label, big advance fees, well-connected publicists, a coordinated tour. But it's more common for even a popular DJ to receive a cease-and-desist order than to get a mix-album deal with a large label.

It's hard to care. Viral culture doesn't play well with intellectual property laws. I knew *Gold Teeth Thief* couldn't enter the commercial world when I did it. I didn't need it to. Word-of-mouth buzz and bootleg mixes are the DJ's symbolic currency; live shows provide the cash. A few months after *Gold Teeth Thief* was posted online, I received my first real gig offer. A choreographer in Berlin wanted to fly me there, house me for a night or two, and pay me €500 to DJ. Good that he didn't haggle over the fee—I would have done it for free. Being paid the equivalent of a month's rent back in Madrid to mix my favorite records! My head spun. Little did I know that this was to be the first of many such offers; *Gold Teeth Thief* ended up being a great calling card.

In the years to come I would start performing in far-flung locales and cosmopolitan megacities: a sprawling, multitiered nightclub in Zagreb, a tiny gallery in Osaka, a former brothel in São Paulo, the American Museum of Natural History. All the while I was crossing paths (and in many cases collaborating) with a huge range of musicians, producers, fans, visual artists, technological visionaries, and fellow DJs from all over the world. Some of these were industry veterans who had toured the globe many times; others were teenagers leaving the confines of their sub-

Saharan villages for the first time in their lives. The bottom line? I saw and learned a lot more than I would have had I stayed put in Massachusetts. Without realizing it, just as the music world was making its fitful, uncertain transition from analog to digital, I was getting a frontline education in the creative upheavals of art production in the twenty-first-century globalized world.

In 2009, almost a decade later, I appeared on a New Yorker Festival panel about the state of the music industry. The magazine had assembled delegates from every cross section of the music biz to weigh in. The panelists included a major-label bigwig, the owner of a prestigious downtown New York independent label, a veteran studio session musician (he'd played bass for everyone from Caetano Veloso to Henry Rollins), and a marketing guru who'd discovered Nirvana—and then me, I suppose as the representative of burgeoning digital culture.

I was the last to speak that afternoon, and I was a bit surprised by all that was said before I had my turn. One by one, everyone else onstage told his or her personalized version of the same story: that in the last decade the sky had fallen—the rise of digital culture had pretty much killed off every aspect of the music business, and we were left to react, defensively, to these harsh changes. Granted, I knew things were bad in a lot of ways. Around 2003 I started to see all my favorite record shops in Manhattan and Brooklyn shutting their doors. CD sales fell dramatically, and distributors and record labels were taking fewer artistic risks. Visionary musicians who for the last decade or two had been able to survive—barely—on a trickle of record-sale royalties were forced into silence and bad day jobs. As the money hunkered down around concerts and merchandise, corporations such as Live Nation started buying up independent venues across the States, replacing fan-built booking networks with a more streamlined, profit-maximizing approach. Ticket prices went up, and while live gigs continued to flourish, those profits didn't necessarily reach the musicians sweating onstage each night. Everyone was a bit worried.

But, at the same time, my experiences have shown me that for each of the avenues closed down by the proliferation of digital technology, unexpected new pathways have opened up.

BIRTH OF A SOUNDBOY

Dancing is a form of listening.

And I wouldn't be a musician if it weren't for nights spent on the dance floor of an after-hours club in Boston called the Loft.

DJs spun house on the first floor. The smaller upstairs room was dedicated to faster stuff, loosely grouped under the category rave music, which mostly meant techno, but at some point they started playing hour-long sets of jungle. It was an epiphany. When I first experienced the Loft DJs' transition from techno's thump-thump-thump clockwork to the percussive mayhem of jungle, it felt as if music had unfolded into a new dimension. Jungle was spacious, edgy, and sudden, built from sliced-up breakbeats spiked with hip-hop and reggae samples. Those bits of other records (many of which I had in my collection) offered concrete footholds into musical history, while the genre as a whole flung itself forward, with fresh mutations and reinventions each month.

I remember feeling submerged as bass lines, blubbery and whaleish, rolled around the room. Sonic activity in the midrange frequencies was often sparse, stepped back to let the low and high ends of the spectrum hit with maximum impact and clarity. Unpredictable kick-and-snare combinations skittered high above the bass, programmed into machine-gone-wild levels of complexity, at twice the tempo. This meant that the dancers could choose which rhythmic time frame to follow: the busy percussion (the speed of fast techno) or the half-time bass line (the speed of slow hip-hop). Mostly we did our best to embody both dynamics, fast and slow, in acknowledgment that this new music was asking us to move in new ways.

During all of this the DJs were nowhere to be seen. Surely they must have been tucked away in some booth somewhere. I never bothered to look for them. It was dark, and who wants to be a wallflower? And what was there to watch even if we found them? The focus was on the sound, as activated by us dancers. We didn't need a figurehead onstage pulling in our attention. There wasn't even a stage. This was music without heroes. We were what was happening.

Those late nights at the Loft taught me never to take an audience for granted. It's not something that just materializes and passively consumes your creation. Especially in the visual arts, there's the sense that an artist makes his or her work, installs it in a gallery, and that's it. Little consideration is given to who's going to see and how they might engage with it. Whereas up in the Loft, engagement with the audience was everything: the crowd responded to the energy of the mix, and the DJs fed off that, creating a tight feedback loop. The audience became a form of intelligence and expression in and of itself. The people in the room were never entirely separate from the performers.

These experiences inspired me to become a DJ. The Loft showed me that I didn't need to jump around onstage or even play an instrument to be a musician. I didn't even have to be seen! Perfect for a shy soundboy. Besides, I'd fallen in love with jungle, and back then the only way to access it outside of the club was to listen to hard-to-get twelve inches, which meant buying them, and if I was gonna do that, I might as well go all the way. I scraped together savings for months to be able to buy a pair of secondhand Technics 1200s turntables from DJ Bruno, one of the residents at the Loft. It turned out to be one of the best purchases I ever made. Two decades later they work as well as they did the day I bought 'em.

Near the beginning of my career, I did a DJ set at the Montreux Jazz Festival, up in the mountains of Switzerland. For me it was crazy. I was DJing in front of a thousand people for the first time, and it was working, they were following me. I was doing what I would do at home, no-holds-barred. Even on that big stage, I stuck to the no-frills performance attitude I learned at the Loft. I don't throw my hands in the air, pump my fist, wave at cute dancers, or yell shout-outs into the mic. I kept my attention trained on the mixer and the turntables, swallowed up in the work, only glancing at the crowd every so often to gauge responses.

Montreux was a predominantly white, European crowd, and I'm a black DJ. (The festival program said I was a woman of Egyptian Italian descent, but we all make mistakes.) A lot of security was up front, and I saw this one other black guy, trying to reach me.

"Hey!" he yelled. "Hey, DJ!" I didn't look up. Ten minutes later he was still there, still gesturing.

I asked security to let him get close so I could hear. "'Back That Azz Up'!" he shouted. "Play 'Back That Azz Up'!" Ten years later, it's no longer a Juvenile song, but perhaps a song featuring a kid from Juvenile's crew—Lil Wayne—that somebody will still shout for, every night, anywhere in the world. That people remain comfortable barking orders at DJs to play this or that song (often fully out of touch with whatever the DJ is mixing at the moment) speaks to the lingering confusion about what a DJ is. Jukebox or creator? Something you become when playing YouTube vids at a house party or a life path that takes years of specialized training?

While this lack of consensus about the role of talent and technique in DJ culture is part of what I find so compelling about it, I like to explain what's going on whenever possible.

Bands perform songs; DJs perform records. With the old techniques—scratching, cutting, beat-matching, and blending—DJs synchronize two records around a common tempo, using a mixer to blend the songs together. The basic mechanics developed in the hip-hop scene of the South Bronx in the 1970s and haven't changed much since. The workhorse turntable, standard in clubs the world over, is still the Technics 1200. The design of this twenty-six-pound behemoth has remained the same since its 1978 debut.

For years I used three turntables. These days my setup has evolved to incorporate two turntables, a laptop, and a robust CD player designed for turntable-like DJ use called a CDJ. Either way, the multiple sound sources playing at once makes the mixing more delicate than the standard two turntables setup. One slip will send the pattern from harmony into *trainwreck*, so-called because the arrhythmic clatter of beats will derail the dance floor. But if you mix right, you can get a single "new" totality whose individual elements can still be heard clearly if you know what you're listening for. A fan who's been watching comes over and says, "I really like that song. What is it?" I can only ask, "Which one?" The DJ's job is to make disparate records sound like a whole, and the more successful you are at it, the less likely the novice onlooker is to know it. DJs have to work to avoid silence and make things appear seamless. You build things up. One of the paradoxes central to the DJ's art is that some of the most demanding, virtuoso work is the hardest to recognize. And some of the highest-paid, most in-your-face DJs do the least amount of actual onstage work.

Fact is, whether you're using record players or CDJs or a tablet, it takes about an hour to show someone the fundamentals of DJing. Live electronic music performers, streaming their own recorded music from laptops, do things differently. They follow the basic template given to us by dub reggae. Take a preexisting song, add effects, momentarily remove (*dub out*) parts. Live electronic dance music (EDM) acts basically mess up their own music, which is prebuilt and then disassembled. The more active they appear, the more the original piece is being interrupted.

Nearly all of us DJs try our hands at making original electronic music. It's tricky. Good DJs must have great taste, but great live DJ mixes are exciting in precisely the way that great original albums aren't: they're heterogeneous, unanticipatable, improvisatory.

Which program you use can affect the product and sometimes nearly determine your genre. The most popular music software in the favelas of Rio de Janeiro and their counterparts across Latin America is ACID (what I started producing music on), a simple application for making sample-based music—great for folks without much musical training. A program called FL Studio, aka FruityLoops, powers most amateur (and plenty of professional) electronic music production across the globe. Max/MSP tends to produce tone clouds of granulated noise. While it's certainly possible to go against the grain when creating with any of these programs (that's how you get the good sounds more often than not), they are comparable to different musical instruments, the way someone strapped into a tuba will be inclined to write different songs than someone bowing the *erhu*, a two-string Chinese fiddle whose characteristic sound derives from its python-skin resonator.

Just as there's a limited number of computer programs that let you make beat-based electronic music, only a few let you

perform it. In the past dozen years, nearly all have been sup-
planted by a popular upstart—Ableton Live. The majority of "live"
dance music acts now use Ableton, won over by its performance-
optimized stability. I grind my teeth when I recognize Ableton's
built-in F/X. That ping-pong filter delay algorithm is so obvious!
It's like pouring ketchup on everything! My friends tell me to
relax. Besides, when I make music I use Ableton more than any
other program.

HAVE RECORDS, WILL TRAVEL

DJed music develops in the great centers: London, New York,
Paris. But the artists make much of their living in forays to
the periphery. And increasingly styles from far-flung corners
of the world are migrating into the Western mainstream. To
state culture bureaus, our music sounds like art and the "avant-
garde," a means of prestige. To kids coming of age in a world
of technology and unhinged capitalism, our music seems to
sound the way global capital is—liquid, international, porous,
and sped up.

Yet our sounds are also a vocabulary for those who detest
the walled-off concentrations of wealth and steal property
back: the collectives that build their own sound systems, stage free
parties, and invite DJs to perform. The international DJ becomes
emblematic of global capitalism's complicated cultural dimension. On flights and at the free continental breakfasts in hotels,

often the same soul-destroying chain hotels in each city, we get stuck chatting with our fellow Americans and Western Europeans, the executives eager to find compatriots. We make small talk with these consultants and deal makers in the descending elevators in the evening—then go out to the city's dead-end and un-owned spaces or its luxury venues to sound-track the night for the region's youth, hungry for something new. DJ music is now the common art form of squatters and the nouveaux riches; it is the sound track both for capital and for its opposition.

Economics favor the DJ. A club can make an event out of one big-name DJ plus local support and pay just the headliner. A popular indie band would need a much higher fee for each member to walk away with similar earnings. Plus it's only one plane ticket and one hotel room for the DJ; each band member ups the cost, and groups often need to drive, need gear rental or roadies, et cetera. Paying marquee DJs six figures for a single performance is not unheard of, especially ever since Las Vegas casinos realized they could cash in on the EDM boom.

The secret of Vegas is that money is boring. Hence all the bluster. Unfortunately that applies to the music nights there too. But only a few dozen DJs worldwide can command those fees, just as only a handful of venues can afford to pay them.

While the dudes at the very top (a woman has yet to enter the *Forbes* annual list of the highest-paid DJs in the world) get paid upward of $2,000 *a minute*, the much more common scenario is that of the DJ who plays for free drinks and cab fare, never earning more than he or she spends on records or audio files.

At the other end of the spectrum lie the improvised venues, the semilegal warehouses, the microcommunities. These anarchic spaces are best understood as alternative social centers, especially in Western Europe, where property laws offer squatters a modicum of legal protection. A thousand people came to the last party that my friend Filastine and I threw in La Makabra. La Makabra sprawled across half a city block in the Barcelona district called Poblenou—"new city," in Catalan. The squat had a gymnasium, library, nursery, skate park, two concert halls, and space for at least thirty people to live. They even had a lawyer. At our party we met Swiss gallerists and homeless kids, all dancing. Six months later the cops evicted the residents (illegally) and bulldozed the place within hours. But Makabras exist all over Europe—in Milan, Paris, Ljubljana.

Between the rich and spiritually vacant venues and the poor and illegally occupied ones are all manner of spaces, from crazy artist-run clubs such as Hamburg's infamous Golden Pudel to countryside festivals with temporary populations the size of a small town (including the teknivals staged by *travelers*, a European hybrid of itinerant ravers, anarcho-punks, and off-the-grid nomads). Not to mention loopholes where economic rules are suspended. Government money for cutting-edge parties? It happens. Impossible things become possible. Dead of winter, somewhere in Austria: we're playing outside—well, technically we're playing *inside* a subzero refrigerated truck parked near an industrial canal. We, the performers, are in one vehicle, and the speakers—and the audience—are in two adjacent trucks, where the thermostats are set as low as they can go. "To avoid possible frostbite and colds," ran the invitation of the art collective that staged the event, "hot mulled wine and baked pea soup are served." I don't remember if the refreshments were free. I can't imagine why they wouldn't have been: everything else was funded by Austrian taxpayers. Arts funding in Europe is like magic dust.

When you're back home, a different kind of magic accompanies the DJ's aura: the easy money of remixes, corporate events, advertising. Twice I've been scheduled to play a gig with a well-known DJ. Twice he's canceled to do a private event. Global brands fly him around the world to entertain at their in-house parties. Since these events pay so well and are so fundamentally uncool, some DJs' corporate earnings far exceed that from their public gigs—but they'll never admit it. A couple of years ago a magazine even flew me across an ocean to play for forty-five minutes. Naked girls on pedestals got their bodies painted, and everybody else shouted at one another over mouthfuls of free sushi.

I do receive plenty of remix offers, courtesy of everyone from an Algerian raï singer to a Spanish girl group asking me to "improve" their number one hit. You can't improve a number one hit by making it better—not in these people's world. When people request remixes, what they really want is to attach a DJ's name to theirs. Aura is contagious; aura rubs off. The music tends to be secondary. So the more money a label offers me to remix, the less time I spend on it. For remix offers of $1,000 and up, my time limit is eight hours of work, start to finish. If I spend any longer, the track will inevitably get more personal and the label people will be less likely to accept it. Besides, eight hours is a lot of time to spend on something that you won't necessarily get paid for. If a label rejects your remix, you can't release it elsewhere, since the label owns the music.

On tour, life becomes simplified. Travel, wait, play, sleep, repeat. Nations blur. Languages splinter; all you need is English. Few musicians bother to learn about the countries they perform in. We're the opposite of tourists. All cities look the same when you arrive at night, get driven to the venue, and leave the next morning. But DJs understand rooms as few others do. You can walk into an empty venue and instantly envision how that night's crowd will react to the architecture of that space.

Both DJing and electronic music production are learned in an artisanal way. One is generally either self-taught or apprenticed. The mechanics of DJing are simple to demonstrate. All you need to do it right are years of practice and the sensitivity of real listening. For the DJ, the actual performance is never just about the musical selection and mixing, something you can work out in advance. The dynamics of the sound system have to be contended with, and how the bodies are reacting to what comes out of it, and what you then have to do about it. When I DJ, I almost never pick out individuals in the dancing crowd. At a good party, the temperature will noticeably heat up when you put on a song that makes people move. You can feel it on your skin even if you don't look up from your decks.

You have to be watchful for the pieces of musical culture that don't translate, even when they come from the places you're playing in. A few years ago I performed in Dubai, part of the United Arab Emirates. I'd mix in a big Arabic tune, but blend it with other rhythms, so that people would hear my mix style cutting up and overlaying the Middle Eastern source records. I slipped a dancehall riddim underneath Egyptian cabdriver *chaabi*, then used a hip-hop breakbeat to bulwark Rachid Taha's remake of Dahmane El Harrachi's exile classic "Ya Rayah." The Lebanese contingent went wild, but a concerned Emirati came up to the booth. "Could you play less Arabic music?" He pointed to two blond Western girls he was getting down with. Arabic language alienated them, whereas the *niggas* and *bitches* of my rap a cappellas made them want to party. I changed course. Toward the end, however, I decided that it was time for a little techno from Morocco's Rif mountains. This high-energy, jubilant stuff takes more than a few nods from Bollywood film music. The song prompted the Scottish club manager to come over with the same request: "Too much Arabic music. Do you mind ending with something in English?" "It's not Arabic," I said, "it's Berber. From North Africa." He shrugged. He later told me that nobody had ever played Middle Eastern music on his night. He'd be able to spin the whole thing into an example of his ecumenical curatorial slant.

In 2006 I moved to New York City after seven years in Spain. My quality of life ratcheted down several notches; my living expenses doubled. I no longer live next door to an active bullfighting ring and have views of the Mediterranean, Gaudí's Sagrada Família cathedral, and the mountains beyond. (At the start of my time in New York, I lived in a room in a shared loft, complete with stunning vistas of the elevated subway line right outside the window. Rent on that Brooklyn room cost approximately as much as that of a family-size apartment in Barcelona.) Staring at my bank account, a strange fact hit home: as an international DJ, the scale of my income is completely uncoupled from the costs of wherever I live. It's inadvisable to live in one of the world's most expensive cities when your workplace is global. Money burns faster here.

Music has always confounded value, although never more so than now, as it sheds its material scarcity and transforms into downloads and streams. It charts a surreal asymptotic curve. At the zero end lie endless amounts of music from artists self-promoting via free downloads and sites such as WFMU's Free Music Archive (exactly what the name says). MP3 shops ask for around ninety-nine cents a song, and while streaming that same song on YouTube is free, subscription streaming services try to pry $10 to $15 out of your wallet each month. For much of the world, music sales happen largely outside of any organized industry. If you want to own some recording, it's the bootleggers or bust. Those transactions usually mean picking up a shaky CD-R or getting a hundred songs beamed to one's device via Bluetooth by some guy in a market.

The album-as-major-statement seems less viable nowadays, anyway. Between the "shuffle" function on MP3 players and the single-song downloads of iTunes and audioblogs, the album's heyday as a sequentially ordered object of contemplation is ending. Two or three laptops died on me this decade. With each death, I thought of the various MP3s lost—and felt lighter. Relief outweighed anxiety. I know stockpilers who download more music than they can listen to. For some, the most beautiful song is the one they haven't heard yet.

It'd be easier to dispense with the notion of albums (and album sales) if Americans were more hip to DJ culture. Unless you're playing weddings or megaclubs, this is a bad country in which to be a DJ. The fees tend to be lower than in Europe, despite the EDM money mirage, and the treatment by venues is almost always worse, not to mention the ubiquity of rock sound systems ill-equipped for dance music. It's not uncommon for DJs and electronic musicians who can draw substantial crowds in middle-size European towns to face half-empty rooms in U.S. cities.

Things are wacky now. We know this. Anyone interested in what comes next must look further afield then the latest listicle on the viability of streaming or the career of Justin Bieber. The giants—the major labels, the indie labels backed by majors, the RIAA on their leash, and so on—took up a lot of resources. I don't want to haggle over how many micro-cents I get paid per stream or other token gestures toward compensation. I want the giants to fall even faster so we can see what weird flowers start blooming in the spaces left vacant.

And whatever the cost, a truly great song is priceless, tapped into something much larger than itself. Deep emotional resonance, the unbuyable sublime. Perhaps you heard it during your first kiss. Or maybe you licensed it for a flavored-beer commercial and got paid six figures to transform a piece of your artistic persona into corporate shill. A great musical experience exceeds any monetary value you could assign it precisely by immersing you in a world where worth is created in radically different ways from what the market teaches us—therein lies the freedom and the rub. If it were otherwise, these sounds we're all chasing would be a lot less beautiful.

Music is a social act. And it's never been healthier, or more chaotic. It's harder to make generalizations, even about the popularity of pop music; instead, people talk about money. Money runs to the people with the least imagination. Power is not creative.

Let's be honest: it's not terribly difficult to get a few years of relative success as a DJ, earning enough money to scrape by, provided you don't mind borderline poverty. A lot of DJs are dabblers, mere hobbyists, so the more you take it seriously, the faster you'll rise. Even in a city such as New York, which has more DJs than Starbucks, a bit of focus and a reasonably fresh musical approach (or invented backstory) is enough to set you apart from the rabble, and you can coast on that for a while.

The difficult thing is to extend that initial impact into a sustainable career. There's no secret recipe for that. Music gives voice to its time, and as the times are always changing, so are the ways to make that music make money. Media attention cycles shorten as musical trends accelerate, with each new flavor yielding a clutch of artists who offer free material online, their sheer numbers slowly pulling entry-level booking fees downward. Hot DJs spend less and less time in demand, especially ones tied to a particular style. As the industry professionalizes, getting close to institutional power, anything from a well-connected manager or Twitter-famous friend makes more difference to one's prospects than any aesthetic moves. MP3 and streaming revenue doesn't compensate for plummeting album sales, which prompts record labels to make highly conservative decisions when signing artists. And let's face it: even if you can survive all this to scrape out a living, do you really want to be playing raves when you're twice as old as the average attendee?

Sometimes I hear musicians talking—grumbling, really—about leaving music. Quitting. Stopping. "This will be my last album," they say, "this will be my last tour, my last big push." It sounds like a threat, but it's never clear to whom the threat is directed if not the musician saying it. Part of me sympathizes: music is the province of the young, and often the more dedicated one is to music, the more difficult it will be to make that music pay in the long term. It is one thing to be sleeping on couches and receiving barely-above-break-even pay as you tour across Europe in your twenties, and entirely another to do the same thing in your forties.

Yet more than anything else, experiencing music as a DJ has proven to me that the zeitgeist, the spirit of the age, is constantly on the move, manifesting in unanticipated ways. Music exceeds us. That's a beautiful thing. There will always be songs to make the world new again and DJs needed to spin them.

2

AUTO-TUNE
GIVES YOU A BETTER ME

"Why are we here?"
"To hear the music."
She raised an eyebrow. "This is music?"
—ANN LECKIE, *Ancillary Justice*

The most important piece of musical equipment of the last twenty years is not an instrument or a physical object. It's a specialized piece of computer software called Auto-Tune and is now used on a staggering 90 percent of all pop songs.

When it debuted in 1997, Auto-Tune was purely corrective: a clever way to bend off-key notes into pitch perfection. This proved especially popular among studio engineers who had to deal with second-rate vocalists. Say the singer recorded a great take but flubbed one phrase; rather than rerecording the whole track, Auto-Tune could fix everything up.

Seasoned audio engineers thought that the inventor, Dr.

Andy Hildebrand, was tricking them when he demonstrated the software. Once they understood that it really did what it claimed to, studio heads flocked to it. Like magic, you could apply Auto-Tune on a problem section in a recording, and—presto!—bad vocals turned good.

Since the software worked by smoothing over the wonky moments in a song, untrained listeners couldn't spot it. The effect stayed well out of the public's notice until a year later, when Cher's producers discovered that drastic Auto-Tune settings could alter her voice to a surprising robotic warble. Far from the naturalistic pitch correction that wasn't meant to be heard, this was a bold new sonic trick. It transformed the human voice into something conspicuously electronic, flamboyantly digitalized. More than a jingle-ready riff or memorable chorus, this was a new *sound*.

Pop loves novelty, so Cher and her producers decided to unleash the first cosmetic (rather than corrective) use of Auto-Tune on the anthemic chorus of her upcoming single, "Believe." When Rob Dickins, the chairman of Warner Music UK, heard a rough mix, he thought the studio boys had gone overboard and demanded that the effect be removed. "Over my dead body," replied Cher. "Don't let anyone touch this track, or I'm going to rip your throat out." The weird effect stayed; the rough mix was approved as the official mix. Her 1998 "Believe" went on to sell more than 10 million copies worldwide, making it one of the most popular singles of all time, and Cher's first number one hit since 1965.

Her studio team struggled to keep the mechanism behind

"the Cher effect," secret, going so far as to lie about how they'd achieved it. Despite their best efforts, producers slowly figured out how to re-create the sound. In 2005 Florida R&B crooner T-Pain released an album in which nearly every track featured shimmering auto-tuned vocals. What Cher pioneered, T-Pain launched into mainstream popularity. Within months T-Pain's giddy robo-choruses had conquered American pop radio.

Since T-Pain, Auto-Tune use spread from singing to, well, just about everything. When confronted with crazy inputs, Auto-Tune tends to generate crazy outputs. Some joker auto-tuned a baby crying and put the audio on YouTube: the eerie results (a musical scream!) spawned countless remixes across West Africa. The Cher effect gave us the first truly new sound of the Internet era. This development was sparked by a fiftysomething pop star and spread like wildfire across genres, languages, and geography. All around the globe, pitch-correction software has reconfigured deep-seated ideas of what humans sound like. Its impact traveled beyond strictly musical culture to become admired—and reviled—worldwide.

Vocal purists hate Auto-Tune. They hear in its robotic modulations some combination of sugar-rush novelty, bulldozed nuance, jejune synthetics, loss of "soul," disdain for vocal talent, teen-optimized histrionics, emotional anemia, and/or widespread musical decline. It's ugly.

Love it or hate it, traditional singing chops aren't so useful in Auto-Tune's world. Years ago after a gig in Paris I made my way out to the *banlieues* to meet one of my favorite Moroccan producers, Wary. After joking about vocalists who ask him to "make their voice robotic," he told me, "Sometimes you have great singers who don't know how to use Auto-Tune and it sounds really bad."

Unlike standard effects such as reverb or distortion, which coat a sound evenly, Auto-Tune actively responds to subtleties in the source material. It doesn't flatten or smooth. Nor does it universalize. Auto-Tune analyzes incoming audio and, depending on what it "hears," responds in radically different ways. In-tune notes may pass through it unaltered, whereas the software will work hard to make wrong notes right. Ari Raskin, chief engineer of high-end Manhattan recording studio Chung King, explains, "If you sing really 'on' [key], then the effect is less drastic."

Raskin has recorded with countless major vocalists, including the bestselling rapper Lil Wayne. Corrective Auto-Tune is everywhere; often the artists themselves won't be aware that the recording engineer has fixed a note or two in the mix. The only way to spot it is to listen for a lack of vibrato. It zaps those natural quavers and tremolos (which happen to be a musical signature of opera).

Cosmetic Auto-Tune, in turn, couldn't be more obvious. Lil Wayne goes so far as to record his raw vocal tracks with Auto-Tune on the whole time—no untreated vocal version exists. In an era of powerful computers that allow musicians to toggle on and off a wide range of effects on vocals after the recording session, recording direct with Auto-Tune entails full commitment because no original "naked" version exists. This is a cyborg embrace.

This interplay between singer, software, and song becomes complex. Vocal runs that would sound bizarre without Auto-Tune have become necessary to create some now-common effects. Far from novelty, Auto-Tune is a contemporary strategy for intimacy with the digital. All this vocal negotiation is neither a fight with technology nor an embrace of it; it's more like glossy coexistence, a strange new dance of give-and-take. Quite literally, this is the sound of voice and machine intermodulating.

Auto-Tune arrived on the world stage at the precise instant when recording studios were completing their shift from hardware to computer-based setups. By the midnineties music software had gotten good enough to emulate the boxy drum machines and keyboards (which themselves were imitating grand pianos, harpsichords, and the like). As the decade progressed, music-making capabilities became increasingly available to anyone with access to a computer and some chutzpah. PCs cost money, sure, but lots of homes had one already. The broke and the curious who could never afford expensive programs such as Auto-Tune could explore the wealth of free and low-cost sound apps, or with a little elbow grease, they could install pirated warez versions of the exact same stuff the pros had. Antares Auto-Tune represented the best of this moment: it was a musical tool with no physical precedent at all. The software did something that had never been possible before.

This new digital creation environment was further strengthened by online distribution. Whether one ordered the CD or found the cracked version hiding deep in Usenet hacker groups,

Auto-Tune became the first musical effect to spread natively in that network space. With hardware, there was always a delay between one's exposure to music made from some new gear or technique and one's access to the tools required to reproduce it. Software contracted that gap. No need to wait for shipping: the lag time between sonic innovation and mainstream uptake all but vanished. A technique pioneered in Los Angeles could be replicated in backwater Uzbekistan studios days later.

With its cyborg effects, digital distribution, and near-instant worldwide reach, Auto-Tune became the first and most emblematic musical tool of the new millennium.

As if to prove the point, the first people I knew of to wholeheartedly embrace Auto-Tune's uncanny technological effects weren't American R&B stars—they were Berber musicians from remote corners of North Africa. Even now, nearly two decades later, Berber Auto-Tune use remains as ubiquitous as it is sonically extreme.

ALL ROADS LEAD TO ROBOTS

Berber songs stroll. They are unhurried even by the languorous standards of Moroccan music. Much North African music uses tempo accelerations or sudden rhythmic shifts to create narrative tension. Berber pop tends toward the long and loping, built around polyrhythms whose metric complexities don't jive with 4/4. Hand claps interlock with the buzzy *bendir* frame drum to create rhythms that the body follows more readily than the head.

Male-female duets are common. Electronic keyboards dialed to trumpet or agile acoustic violins mirror the call-and-response vocals. One of the strongest branches of this music is built around spacey, extended banjo melodies.

These are sturdy songs, upholding a tradition where repetition trumps change. Yet starting around 2000, I began to notice the presence of what I would later recognize as Auto-Tune. This was almost immediately after Cher, and years before anybody except Tallahassee rap fans had heard of T-Pain.

Within a few years, it was impossible to find an album of Berber folk-pop where the vocals *weren't* drenched in synthy Auto-Tune. The most striking songs were the ones in which all the instrumentation was acoustic—drums, guitars, hand claps—everything, that is, except the voices. The vocals on these tracks were saturated with full-on cyborg Auto-Tune. I grew fascinated that, out of all the broadly Western influences that could have been adapted into this music (from beat patterns to fashion choices), the Cher effect was the only one that passed muster. It's the equivalent of rural bluegrass singers across Appalachia suddenly starting to use Auto-Tune while doing everything else the old-timey way with banjos and fiddles and washtub percussion.

Questions piled up that no amount of online research or conversations at Moroccan shops in Europe could answer. I booked a flight to Casablanca to look for answers.

Within the Maghreb region of Africa—the vast swath of land sweeping from Libya to Mauritania—Morocco is probably the

most highly developed: modern highway systems installed over
the past decade have halved driving time between major cities;
the Atlantic coastline bristles with cranes and high-rises as
foreign investors fuel development. With its 4 million inhabitants, Casablanca is easily the largest, most cosmopolitan city of
the Maghreb's six countries. Given this, driving into the nearby
Berber territories feels like spooling back centuries. In the hundreds of towns and villages dotted across the landscape, ancient
rhythms of life still hold sway.

Ranging back almost three thousand years, the indigenous
Berber people have always lived in a kind of willful isolation
from whichever ethnic or national group was in charge of Morocco. Over the centuries, waves of invaders have tried to alter
the hard-to-reach Berbers, from Romans to Arabs bearing Islam
to the colonizing French of the nineteenth and twentieth centuries, who granted independence fifty years ago, leaving the country ruled by an Arab elite. Today roughly 11 million indigenous
Berbers—a third of Morocco's people—live in thinly populated
clusters across some of North Africa's most inhospitable terrain:
the marijuana-producing Rif mountains of the north, the wind-
lashed Atlas Mountains in the country's center, and the southern Anti-Atlas range, which shores up against the Sahara Desert.
These challenging landscapes command respect. Even the architecture of the Berber village emphasizes its separatism. Whereas
Morocco is known internationally for its mazelike medinas and
bustling public squares, Berber architecture reflects a proud
and defensive cultural stance: the walled city, the fortified houses,
the communal granaries, and the watchtowers.

For millennia Berbers have referred to themselves as Amazighs, which means "free people." The Romans simply called them "barbarians." Unfortunately for the Amazighs, the word stuck; an ancient "barbaric" stigma remains. Even though Berber—they call it Tamazigh—is the main language spoken in much of the country, it was illegal to teach or print until the early twenty-first century. As recently as the mid-1990s, people were getting thrown in jail for staging Berber cultural festivals or using the language in public theater performances.

In recent decades, the age-old mutual antipathy with the Arab ruling class spurred a new wave of Berber migration from Morocco to Europe. This meant that I had the chance to hear a lot of current Amazigh music at Muslim bars in the red-light districts of such cities as Marseilles, Brussels, and especially Barcelona during my five years there. This time was priceless to me because I'd always loved what little Berber music I'd been able to hear.

Forget "Play it again, Sam." Casablanca is an utterly modern, unromantic city that has nothing to do with the movie that bears its name. Here even the beautiful buildings are made from concrete. Casablanca repels tourists while attracting hungry young men from the countryside looking for work. Traffic-choked roadways connect upscale neighborhoods to shantytowns whose residents have satellite dishes but no running water. The country's music industry headquarters is here, sandwiched between those extremes.

My friends Hassan Wargui and Abdellah Kabbani, gifted

yet luckless Amazigh musicians, join up with me—partly to help
with translation, partly for the thrill of an odd chase. A short
bus ride from the city center delivers us into the hyperkinetic
shopping chaos of the Hay Amal neighborhood. Sidewalk vendors overtake a few lanes of Avenue Mohammed VI on bigger
market days, halving the vehicular flow in one of the city's rare
concessions to its millions of beleaguered pedestrians. Everything one could want is being sold: toothpaste, live birds, amateur dentistry services, ink-jet-pixelated assembly-line paintings
replicating nineteenth-century French orientalist tableaux, elaborate lingerie of Syrian origin, George Eliot paperbacks, paint,
broth-boiled snails picked off thistles in the city's rubbly vacant
lots—all without a price tag. Like reality itself here, the value of
goods is established by intense discussion between the buyer
and the seller, two people if not more, amoebic concentrations
of onlookers and friends and busybodies, any of whom might
speak to the matter being negotiated.

As we walk down the avenue, bustling street commerce
congeals into the hardscrabble market known as Souk Layoum.
"This is the heart of Casablanca," announces Abdellah as he
gestures toward the odd piles of is-it-trash-or-is-it-for-sale?
decorating the entrance. "The heart of the city is a very dirty
place." Abdellah has forgotten what little Mandarin he picked up
while working in a Chinese-run factory; places such as Layoum
operate as a direct portal to Chinese-manufactured schlock,
which saturates these markets as it does similar ones across the
global South. The inorganic tang of injection-molded plastics

off-gassing complex, probably carcinogenic polymer molecules mingles with sweat and diesel exhaust—welcome to the true embassies of the world. Find the sellers of cheap plastic and you'll have found the sellers of music, because for most of the world music is only worth as much as the plastic it comes delivered on. A fraction of a dollar for hundreds of songs crammed on as MP3s.

A handful of the smaller labels that call this neighborhood home know me by now—I'm that strange American who materializes once or twice a year to buy music that nobody has considered exporting. One of my favorite labels, Sawt Nassim, lies inside a dimly lit Layoum warehouse. Familiarity has forged something resembling friendship between the owner, Khalid, and me, though you wouldn't know it by listening to our conversations, which consist primarily of me asking questions, then waiting a few seconds until Khalid gives me a name or a phone number, grunts yes or no, or simply stares at me in silence until I ask something else.

Khalid releases the music of Adil El Miloudi. Throughout my time in Morocco I repeatedly found myself in conversation with otherwise pleasant individuals who passionately tried to convince me that the work of the greasy and piggish entertainer El Miloudi was not music but noise—multiple people, men and women, used that word, *noise*—so with due respect for my interest I should be researching someone else. No matter. I'd been impressed with Adil ever since I'd heard him, unattributed, on a bootleg compilation in a Paris store where a flock of hijab-wearing urbanites laughed at me in scorn for requesting it. Years later I connected a name to the voice, only to discover how popular he was. When Adil opens his mouth, gruff golden melodies pour out. Some of his biggest hits employ social-realist lyrics, chromed in Auto-Tune, to elevate the travails of the underclass without being depressing or didactic.

Adil El Miloudi regularly performs for Moroccan communities across Europe and holds down a residency at a Tangier nightclub called the Morocco Palace. Entrance is free—they gouge you on *shisha* and drink prices. The Palace has a light-up disco dance floor and good subwoofers. Everything else is covered in intricate Islamic-pattern plasterwork, except the enormous flatscreen TV right above the stage, which is set to a music-video channel and is never, ever turned off, not even when live bands are playing underneath it. Adil and his fellow singers don't use Auto-Tune here. Only a few well-funded Moroccan festivals are equipped to do it live.

Halfway between Casablanca and the northern outpost of Tangier lies the coastal town of Kenitra, where Adil lives with his wife and two sons. He rolls around town with a phalanx of young guys whose primary duty seems to be handing him various cell phones at the appropriate moment. I know this because, after calling several of those phones from Casablanca and being led through some enormous travel missteps, I found myself at Adil's house at two in the morning. "This is Tom," he said, pointing at his manager. "And this is Jerry," he said, pointing at his cat.

Eventually I brought the conversation around to Auto-

Tune. Why is it so popular in these parts? "Auto-Tune gives you a better me," said Adil without missing a beat. This sly epigrammatic wisdom is part of what keeps him in demand as a lyricist (for other artists). The phrase became a mantra echoing throughout my time in Morocco: *Auto-Tune gives you a better me.*

The following week I meet with Amazigh singer Jamila Tamntaght at Les Fleurs, a dark downtown Casablanca café done up in worn 1960s bachelor-pad futurism. Around the corner the complex codes of prostitution in the city flash in and out of visibility, with many sex workers' nights ending in mornings here inside, but the mood and meaning of the place depend very much on the time of day. Jamila arrives with her husband, Khalid Wakrim, who serves as bandleader. He's skinny, reserved, and dark skinned, wearing an instantly forgettable shirt-and-pants combination like every other man in Les Fleurs. She's plump, exquisite, and outspoken, dressed in a fine black djellaba that sets off her pale complexion. The middle-aged parents move together like newlyweds. They radiate the same light.

Of all the musicians I meet in Morocco, Tamntaght strikes me as the most even-keeled. She plays by the rules, and the game sustains her. She's not a star like Adil El Miloudi, but work is steady, split between music and acting in the fledgling Amazigh movie industry. Over the next hour, our conversation presented what would grow to become a refrain when I talked to musicians—in the scant time that it's been around, Auto-Tune has comfortably established itself in the studio toolbox.

Of course she records with it. Not all the time, mind you, but often. Who doesn't? It's an industry standard! It's nearly not worth talking about, and how about if we discuss business practices or her upcoming film role or watch some of her music videos instead?

The charismatic singer commandeers my laptop to load videos on her Facebook page. We crowd around the screen to watch Jamila smiling into the camera by a cascading river, Jamila wearing traditional fineries in a rug-covered room, Jamila in a jumpsuit and beret next to a palm tree, Jamila with her hair curled up in Princess Leia buns—all in one song. The changes of scene and dress tell no story beyond cycling through different portrayals of modest contemporary Berber womanhood. In video after video, there are no urban images. The closest thing we get is a shot of Tamntaght on a rocky outcrop looking down on the city of Agadir. She's not alone in this studied avoidance of the urban. It's a common feature of Berber music videos and album artwork. Musicians who have lived their entire lives in Casablanca will travel for a day or two to shoot videos in the southern Berber wilderness, such is the importance of this pastoral branding. The Amazigh musical imagination shuns the city as much as American hip-hop avoids the rural.

A different waiter refills our tea. He too is Berber. Much is made of this happy coincidence. Speaking Tamazigh here links one to a community of people, overwhelmingly male, whose lives stretch awkwardly between the unkind metropolis and their jobless home villages. The experience of exploring Casablanca with Amazighs passports you into a second, contemporaneous city, one much smaller and friendlier and closer to the countryside.

After the video-fest Jamila updates her Facebook status with news of the interview. Incoming chat requests bloop at us, and I wonder if our digital appendages will grow louder and more insistent, first bleeping then *sssshst*-ing and nay-saying and eventually shouting us down when we don't lavish on them the attention they feel they deserve. All my Berber acquaintances in Morocco love Facebook, to the ridiculous extent that in their social circle you don't "go online," you "go to Facebook." Facebook is bigger than the whole world here, and the Internet fits right inside it. This is the familiar story of the digital swallowing us into its belly, but among the Amazigh there's a twist: Facebook boots up into a city-within-the-city, a precious online village where everything is written in Berber, this corner of the global mediascape that they can call their own.

Jamila suggests we stop by Studio Moulouk, where she's recording her album. I leap at the chance. When I visited Moulouk the year before, head engineer Abdelkrim graciously demonstrated how he uses Auto-Tune. Then he held my gaze: "Only bad singers need this. You know that, right?" Now we're taxiing back with an artist who does not share such prejudice.

After a brief reintroduction, Abdelkrim boots up Cubase (the main audio production program in recording studios across most of Africa) and opens the draft of Jamila's upcoming single. Waves of happy, high-energy pop flood the control room. Jamila does the peppy shoulder dance. She lip-synchs her lyrics, then decides (correctly) that everyone within earshot needs to dance. Song becomes celebration. We're dancing on the threadbare carpet. To someone unmoved by this power of music, we're simply a bunch of people, strangers to each other, gathered in a drab and windowless studio where dead roaches the size of your thumb litter the floor, poor in most senses of the word. But this song pushes out the walls of the room, lets in sunlight. Jamila urges everyone to hold hands, everyone except Abdellah, who is busy filming us on his phone (Facebook might want to see this). Auto-Tune is less than automatic. Karaoke is more than imitation. Participate. It is open. Bodies joined in dance are what give the music meaning. A five-minute pop song puts all other clocks on hold. We are the richest people in the world, perhaps the only people, right now.

Abdelkrim plays it cool. He's paid to give customers what they want. Which, here, means fifteen years of Auto-Tune and rising. Left to his own devices, Abdelkrim wouldn't touch the software. The arc of every recording studio must be like this—someone starts it for love of not music *in general* (never trust people who tell you that they "like music"), but a particular kind of music in a particular moment. The zeitgeist moves on. Maybe you flow with it, maybe not.

The transformation of twenty-first-century music production from expensive hardware studios to a haphazardly democratic scatter of home computers has made it possible for bare-bones studios such as Moulouk to exist. That same wave of studio digitization lodged Auto-Tune software firmly in the global pop toolbox. Something distinct in Maghrebi listening habits keeps it there in near-constant use.

WHITNEY

Forgive a detour—I think a careful listen to Whitney Houston may bring us closer to understanding what's going on in Maghrebi listening habits.

"I Will Always Love You," one of the world's most popular singles, was written by Dolly Parton in 1973. Even Elvis Presley wanted to record a cover version. His legal team demanded that Parton give him half the songwriting credit. This was their standard strong-arm offer (most artists happily ceded 50 percent of songwriting profits to Elvis since he guaranteed sales), and wisely, Parton refused. "I Will Always Love You" was a bona fide moneymaker well before Houston's 1992 rendition for *The Bodyguard* sound track skyrocketed to become the all-time bestselling single by a female artist.

Houston begins unaccompanied, as if the string section and other instruments have, like me, been stunned into silence by the quality of movement inside the filigreed pathways of her voice. Houston doesn't stretch each word out so much as give it wings to fly around in. *I* and *you*—these brief words can last for seconds here, long enough to make sure we all know just how large they really are. The vulnerability of her naked voice ups the bravura. It's a tightrope walk without a safety net (Auto-

Tune hadn't been invented yet). As with Cher's Auto-Tune inno-vation, the record company executives were dead set against the now-famous a cappella opening. It took protests from Houston and *Bodyguard* costar Kevin Costner to keep it intact. (Tone deafness or outright hostility toward music as an art form may not be required to land a job as a major-label exec, but all indications suggest that they sure won't hurt your chances.)

From the outset, Parton's lyrics and melody become sec-ondary to Houston's modulations on them. Whitney inserts pauses, extends syllables, redraws the melody to fit the moment. Her arabesque vocalizations become something in their own right, codependent and contingent yet emotionally, viscerally, musically real. The ornament swells to become the heart.

These effects flow from her masterful use of a technique called melisma. Technically speaking, melisma occurs when vocalists use melodic embellishment to extend a single syllable. Emotionally, it's something else entirely, a mode of expression that bucks against the very limits of language. Indeed, the crush-ing power of "I Will Always Love You," its meaning in sound, results from how Houston's melisma activates a mysterious, even mystical relationship between overflowing emotion, life's vicissitudes, and ultraprecise self-control. Rather than simply sing *about* the bittersweet conflicts involved in saying goodbye to a lover, Houston deploys melisma to enact in sound a heart-felt struggle between holding on and letting go. Like life as it unfurls, each moment is unanticipatable until it happens, whereupon we can't possibly imagine it any other way.

Such is the power of melisma. The technique breathes life-flow into fixed text. Melisma is vocal embellishment's purest form, almost always improvised and therefore rarely written down. Melisma locates meaning in the instant. It reveals to us the risk and control of a singer at her most unpredictably alive.

That the richness Whitney Houston brings to "I Will Always Love You" cannot be written down, owned, or repeated does virtually nothing to prevent *X Factor*, *American Idol*, and related-franchise contestants from doggedly attempting to re-create her solo by rote. Houston's many imitators value the technical virtuosity required to reenact her singular performance—slavishly tracing her melismatic curves turns that freedom into a rule book, against which one can be judged and found wanting. Houston sang it differently each time. Her improvisations focus our attention on the part that is unscripted and unforeseeable.

"I Will Always Love You" was great from the start. Whitney Houston made it a classic. By activating broad words and simple song structure with what sounds like spontaneous, deeply personal utterances, Houston's melisma collapses the space separating intimate and universal. Only the finest pop can lead us to such a place.

Melisma straddles genres and singers and nation-states. I knew it first in black American music such as R&B and gospel. It's positively huge across the Maghreb. Bawdy folksingers, throats burned by a lifetime of whiskey. Honey-voiced Koranic reciters who "sing" the Koran magnificently yet consider all music to be sinful. It doesn't matter who you are or what scene you're in, you're gonna have a tough time if your voice can't flutter around those notes with the grace of a bird and the hairpin turns of a butterfly. Maghreb audiences of all stripes are keyed in, listening to precisely those moments when the voice glides through notes.

Melismatic vocals have formed an integral part of the sonic landscape across huge swaths of Africa, Southeast Asia, and the Middle East for centuries—public recitation of the Koran and the five-times-daily call to prayer rely heavily on the technique. If melismatic styles weren't already widespread, they ended up that way when Islam swept in six hundred years after the birth of Christ. Several musicologists assume that it's what ushered melisma into black American church music and eventually into the bloodstream of an eleven-year-old junior gospel choir soloist named Whitney in the first place.

What does the computer think of this weightless technique of vocal gymnastics whose touch of the divine spans religions? Auto-Tune hates it. For all its algorithmic fineries, Auto-Tune cannot distinguish between world-class melismatic pitch control and off-key drunken shouting. To fix the problem of "out-of-tune vocals," Dr. Hildebrand had to encode into the software his beliefs about what constituted appropriate singing. Auto-Tune hears the opening section of "I Will Always Love You" as one long error in need of digital correction. And it's not just her.

Melisma's swoops and dives are exactly the type of melodic movement that provokes Auto-Tune into extreme corrective mode, thereby producing its most unusual sounds. This, I believe, explains the software's mind-boggling success in North Africa. The region embraced Auto-Tune so early and so heartily because for more than a millennium audiences have been listening to—and for—those gorgeous, subtly rising and falling pitches. And they sound especially startling when processed through Auto-Tune. The familiar pitch slide gets activated by bizarre effects. A weird electronic warble embeds itself in rich, throaty glissandi. The struggle of human nuance versus digital correction is made audible, dramatized in a zone of heightened attention. Listening habits from the dawn of Islam helped Auto-Tune mean so much here.

AMAZIGH IDOL

While melisma helped to explain Auto-Tune's popularity in the Maghreb, I still wondered why the technique hit the Berber areas of Morocco the hardest. The best way to find out was to visit its heart.

Agadir, crown jewel of the Amazighs, lies on the country's southwest coast. Berber culture enjoys majority status here. In 1960 an earthquake destroyed much of the then-small city. Roughly a quarter of its inhabitants died. Agadir's reconstruction drew on French urbanism to create a cleanly modernist, wide-avenued city prized by Moroccan Berbers as their unofficial capital. Budget flights and newly constructed highways have dramatically increased Agadir's accessibility in recent years. Tourism money radiates outward from its miles-long beach, where sun-stunned Europeans wash up year-round.

The Abattoir neighborhood hunkers down near enough to the beach to host flocks of kids dressed to swim or surf, yet far enough away to offer no relief from the heat, with the result that this busy working-class quarter feels more like a desert way station than a seaside vacation town. Banged-up Mercedes cars of indeterminate age crowd the taxi plaza at its heart, ringed by sawdust-floored eateries filled with men and haunted by cats.

Al-Maarif Studio lies behind a nondescript door on the plaza's edge. I am here to get grounded. Some studios transmit the clinical time-is-money tang of a doctor's office; others try to make you feel at ease. Al-Maarif is one of the good ones. An assistant ushers us into the front salon. The openness of Moroccan interior space makes it a joy to wait in. Firm long, low rectangular cushions line the walls. These possibility-rich slabs of furniture can easily seat a dozen people or serve as beds for a handful. A television fastened to the wall plays old Japanese anime. Cartoon people bounce and ripple lysergically, their bodies as flexible and indestructible as folk songs.

The assistant returns with what must be our fourth or fifth sweet mint tea of the day. The welcoming offer of tea means more than the drink itself, particularly for newcomers such as me. I abstractedly cradle my cup, wondering how this country does not suffer from diabetes given the glacier-size chunks of sugar that everybody stirs into their drinks. In lax pastry shops, bees or wasps swarm glazed postcolonial croissants, as addicted to sweeteners as we are. I take another sip. If, like cats, we humans couldn't taste sugar, then eating cookies would be punishment and, lacking reasons for New World sugarcane plantations, the whole history of slavery would have come out differently, at least a nudge less bitter. I drain my cup.

Moments later we're led down a spiral staircase into the basement recording suites. Al-Maarif contains histories, because what do you throw out? Nothing. Five decades of recording equipment sediment the control room. A reel-to-reel tape deck that's older than I am perches near a DAT machine, that soon-obsolete relic of 1990s hi-fi. Somewhere a cricket chirps. A wall clock inscribed with Koran verses presides over it all, the swooping grace of its Arabic calligraphy a visual counterpart to melisma's curves.

Engineer El Hajj Ali Ait Bouzid captains a swivel chair. He walks me through various projects to explain how musicians integrate Auto-Tune into their creative process. First, the backing band records their material. The engineer takes a few days to edit together the best selections and tidy things up, then the singer will come in to lay her raw vocals on top. Finally, the engineer will go in after that, to mix it all together, and *that's* when Auto-Tune creeps in.

In a typical Amazigh combo, the banjo (a notoriously fickle instrument that is constantly going out of tune due to microchanges in ambient temperature and humidity) sets the reference note, the rest of the band tunes to the banjo, and the singer, days later, adjusts her intonation to fit the band. Auto-Tune then gets tuned—or rather, detuned—to whatever results. I say *detuned* because in studios across Morocco, I watched time and again as the people who used Auto-Tune the most relied the least upon its interface. The software offers many ways to customize its effects, including settings called Arabic and Pentatonic—registers that wouldn't be hard to tailor-fit to Berber songs. Nobody bothers with any of that. Instead, people click a single knob—Pitch—and twist. Ait Bouzid and others simply listen to the vocals and adjust the software on the fly, using broad, impressionistic settings until things start to sound the right kind of wrong.

After a few hours listening to electronically enhanced voices genied out of Al-Maarif's hard drive, I realize that there is no cricket. The Koran clock is chirping realistically. I mistook a machine's error for natural sounds while listening to a machine mistake natural sounds for human error. What future awaits us? What future is already here?

Back in the Abattoir streets I spot trilingual posters (written in Arabic script, Roman letters, and Tifinagh, a two-thousand-year-old Tuareg alphabet adopted by the Berbers) advertising albums by heavily photoshopped young women decked out in traditional Amazigh dress. Bingo. These demure girls would lead me to Auto-Tune. I knew this because the robot voice signifies differently everywhere you go, and here in Agadir it is synonymous with wedding music and high-gloss pop, whereas just a few hours south, in the Sahel, Auto-Tune can be hard to find, its use largely confined to a few aspiring rappers.

One phone call and a sweet mint tea later I meet with the singers' manager, Mohammed El Khattaby. Poster girls Fatima Tachtoukt and Saadia Tihihit are his main artists right now. Tachtoukt has three commercially successful albums under her belt, whereas Tihihit's debut CD was released just two weeks ago. Like Justin Bieber or any other child groomed to be a media star, Saadia Tihihit occupies a place at least initially defined more by the commercial strategies of those around her than by any desire for artistic autonomy. She won a local radio station's call-in contest for best amateur singer a few months ago. That led to a management deal with Khattaby, whose job is to telescope that paltry exposure into a career.

The true face of Berber teen pop may well be this watchful, unemotive man with a face like an avuncular wasp. He chooses their songs, assembles the backing band, coordinates publicity, books shows, and bankrolls it all. Similar faces crouch behind every aspiring professional singer. A good management team will present a minimal public profile, if any. After all, their duty is to maximize the appearance that their employer is an individual, unique, brilliant artist. This is singer as mouthpiece. Rihanna is an extreme example—forty-five songwriters are credited on her 2012 album *Unapologetic*. Where does the creative process end and the human resource department begin? Rising stars don't need talent; they need a high-functioning management team.

At Khattaby's request, the following day we meet with his protégées at a café specializing in European-style prices. I'm longing for the Slaughterhouse's sidewalk food joints, where a perfect breakfast of flat bread, argan oil, and almond butter costs as much as this leaden croissant. Our meeting is awkward from the start. There's desperately little outlet for any music journalism in Morocco, and Amazigh coverage forms a sliver of that tiny world. The Moroccans have no real reference for what this artist interview might accomplish, which creates an uneasy tension. *What does the American want?* I imagine them wondering. *Is this a lucky opportunity or a waste of time?* I try to keep the vibe relaxed. Everyone is on his or her best behavior, which leads to such self-policing that speech gets whittled down to platitudes. The result reminds me of interviewing famous rappers who've learned to say nothing as a result of being blasted in the press for saying too much.

Tachtoukt, Tihihit, and Khattaby are seated in a row, and despite my best efforts, they turn into a single creature, a complex three-headed being at pains not to offend or contradict itself. Here's how it works: I ask the girls a general question, and Khattaby answers. I ask a specific girl a specific question, and Khattaby answers. I say, "Now, Khattaby, I'd like to know what Saadia thinks," and he nods, then she nods, muttering a quick answer, while her shyness makes her look down at the greasy crusts of our breakfast as if they contained all the sadness in the world.

Saadia Tihihit is a poor kid from up in the mountains. She owns no cell phone, doesn't get online much, yet ever since she was a toddler, extremely auto-tuned Berber pop has been around. Whatever Tihihit's thoughts are on Auto-Tune and/or the music industry, I'm determined to hear them. As we wrap up the interview, my buddy Hassan finagles her home phone number without Khattaby realizing it so we can set up an unsupervised interview in the hope that she'll speak more freely when he and Tachtoukt aren't there.

That night Khattaby phones Hassan in a rage. "Only an immoral Muslim would sneak an appointment with the young woman behind my back!" Hassan's deep religiosity does not conflict with his highly developed sense of mischief nor does it dampen his pride, the atavistic pride of a handsome single musician. Hassan winds up Khattaby by rattling on about how Hassan could have his pick of any of the single ladies in his village, every last one of them far more beautiful than Saadia and twice as modest to boot! I experience this argument as a blur of rapid-fire Tamazigh punctuated by Hassan's indignant harrumphs. It's clear even from his tinny voice crackling through the phone that Khattaby is hysterical. Beyond consolation. The thing is broken. It's ridiculous. All I wanted was a chaperone-free interview . . . Then it hits me. This macho wrangling over propriety and womanhood has served up a vital clue as to why the Berbers embraced Auto-Tune more fully than their equally melismatic counterparts across the Maghreb.

Ladies shout all over Berber music. Voices sharper than an early-morning chill that can reach across a mountainside, screechy, cutting voices that don't sing so much as declare. "High pitch and loud volume," explains one academic specializing in Berber culture from this region, evoke "female features valued by the collective (although absent in stereotypes of the ideal Islamic woman): confidence, boldness, assertiveness, and bravado." It's an Amazigh thing.

You hear it loud and clear in classic eighties singers such as Fatima Tihihit—on Saadia's debut album, she performs two of Fatima's songs, and three or four singers since have adopted the name to milk the confusion. The clarion call powers contemporary favorites such as Hafida too. Hafida's gifted with a soprano that Auto-Tune liquefies into a bright neon stream, as if a dial-up modem and a river have fallen in love and begun writing violin concerti for each other. Enchanted by her music and curious about her all-female backing band (a rarity in these parts), I put Hafida at the top of my To Find list when I arrived in Morocco. But it was not to be. "Militant," reported Hassan. I'd asked him to research her whereabouts and he'd hit a serious wall. "She married a militant man. No interviews. No music. Finished." I was crestfallen. I'd arrived a few years too late. The in-demand wedding-song specialist got hitched to a conservative husband who forbade her to sing. Was it worth it? Music is an unkillable thing, yet the lives of musicians who give it expression are always so fragile.

As in Jamila's videos or the slick posters for Khattaby's artists papering Agadir, the countryside remains where Amazigh culture most recognizes itself. At the center lies the figure of the rough-yet-pure countryside woman who stands for all things Berber and beautiful. The same happens with her language.

Tamazigh speakers in the city gravitate toward a cosmopolitan median that everyone can more or less understand, yet since Tamazigh comes in wildly different dialects in its many unconnected hinterlands, Berbers scattered around the country without access to the citified version can rarely understand each other. So the least socially mobile Berber women, the ones most isolated from interactions with mainstream Moroccan society, are considered to possess Tamazigh language skills of an unsurpassed, even talismanic beauty, free from corrupting accents and bastardizing Arabisms.

For at least a hundred years now, Amazigh men have been

disappearing to the city for work, leaving their womenfolk to raise families and tend fields in the village. These realities emerge as perennial themes in Berber music. Far from the city's taint, the traditional carrier of linguistic, artistic, and many other types of purity is the Amazigh woman.

Hafida was the exception that proved the rule: she was an Arab Moroccan who learned Berber, then sang in it. Her slight Arabic accent further endeared her to the Amazighs. Where else would one experience an Arab adopting Berber language, dress, culture? As an Arab respectfully engaging with "barbarian" musical culture—for some reason I'm imagining Fox News anchors speaking in a slow Southern drawl—Hafida embodied the possibility of Amazigh globalization: the regional, minority culture bending the mainstream. As we wait for that world to come into being, industrious salesmen in Agadir continue to recycle old Hafida songs on bootleg compilations such as *Amazigh Best of 2016!*

Cultural distinctness, female purity, unblemished nature, and Auto-Tune. Women may not always be directly responsible for applying the effect, yet their voices consistently receive the most extreme auto-tuning in Berber pop. Even in male-female duets, the lady always has her voice more altered, often beyond legibility.

Auto-Tune activates deep-seated and conservative ideals of Berber womanhood by making those high-pitched voices cut even more keenly. The software amplifies old ideas of the rural and the feminine. Music made with it enjoys widespread, lasting popularity. Shockingly contemporary sonic radicalism grafts onto long-standing ideas about gender.

The processed female voices in Berber pop are unavoidably spectacular, yet their pleasures are not precisely of the flesh. With the software, one can simultaneously flaunt that rough-and-pure womanhood while preserving its modesty via a synthetic veil. The cyborg sheen makes bodies less carnal. This hiding and showing at the same time is part of how Amazigh Auto-Tune functions culturally and sonically. It parallels the main Koranic arguments for the veil: "so that they may know who you are" and "to hide your charms from their eyes."

Strong, thin wires link Dr. Andy Hildebrand to Jamila Tamntaght and Saadia Tihihit. The hypnotic sidewinder curves of melisma have held us in thrall for ages. Add to that Internet-era pleasures of hearing these humanity-affirming melodic improvisations interrupted by a clunky software algorithm. The shrill perfect-lady stereotype becomes even more shrill, more perfect, more ladylike. Berber Auto-Tune acts something like a digital veil to protect—and project—a woman's purity as she makes her way in the modern world. No one person is pulling at these wires. We're all a little strung out along them.

My time in Morocco taught me how diffuse Auto-Tune has become. Like a software preset or an unquestioned bias, it's just *there* until you point it out, at which point people deny any direct involvement. *Auto-Tune got on the song, someone asked for it, another expected it, this is how things sound, most of the time . . .*

Widespread notions about the ideal Berber woman simultaneously power and tame Auto-Tune's digital weirdness in Berber Morocco. The Cher effect isn't a single thing but a hydra, angling across ragtag networks where bodies can melt or morph at the press of a button. Will all that is truly new about Auto-Tune be able to shake up cobwebbed social circuitry? Software programs us. One hopes that we can in turn learn to program it in order to better navigate the cyborg present. Nowadays pop arrives everywhere at once. Stronger than language, its sound hits before the words do.

In pushing the American software to the limits with such dedication and flair, the Amazigh have elevated the struggle between human and machine into artistic expression, with all the history of how hard it is to be a woman, here or anywhere, embedded in it at unsettling angles. Auto-Tune sound-tracks the twenty-first-century Amazigh condition, that of a bucolic nation made real only in its digital diaspora. Villagers subsisting with a minimum of state infrastructure (tax inspectors yes, phone lines and garbage pickup no, in many cases) suddenly enjoy smartphones linked to satellite Internet. Ancestral ties strengthen—on Facebook. Auto-Tune is a compelling call-and-response between pastoralist and robot, although nobody's steady enough to point out who is who.

Underneath it all, the mute fact of Saadia's failed interview reminds me of another, harder-to-hear silence, one contained in her music and made possible by all that amplification and exaggeration. Will the electrified have-nots, the Saadias of the world, be able to rewire their own digital reflections and have a say in the networks along which they spread?

My journey across Morocco was sparked by a shimmer in pop that caught my ear and refused to let go. "That stupid effect," said one friend; "the sound that makes me think of capitalism's evils," said another. Cher and Adil El Miloudi had other things to say. If one thread weaves through all the wildly disparate uses of Auto-Tune, it is a tacit understanding that technology slips into us at the messy intersection of pleasure and control, and that the voice itself—individual, fragile, and capable of being made grand or muted in any number of electronic ways—sings out at the heart of the contest between what we've inherited and what we may yet become.

3

HOW MUSIC TRAVELS

If globalization didn't exist, MP3s would have needed to invent it.

The speed with which digital audio zips from one place to another has shrunk the world, short-circuiting business models and scrambling lines of influence. The overwhelming availability of music that results from this proliferation and portability is altering our conception of it in ways we're only beginning to understand. This I know: my tour travels in the early 2000s were kick-started by a paradigm shift in how music itself moves around.

I got invited to DJ all over the globe without having anything remotely like a hit single or video. No label, album, radio play, or publicist either. I couldn't even convince record stores to stock my *Gold Teeth Thief* mixtape on consignment. What I had back in 2001 was an MP3 download link on a boring little webpage, and much to my surprise, that was enough. I found this out when my friend Trieu e-mailed me in Madrid to say that the page he'd set up to host the files had a spike in traffic that wasn't going away. While the raw material for my performances was music I'd personally sourced on vinyl, what I did was traveling in another format entirely: the low and mighty MP3.

A few years before, Trieu became the first person I knew to download an MP3. He grabbed Chuck Berry's "Downbound Train" from some Usenet site and listened to the song over and over, marveling at how something so small could sound so full. The same Chuck Berry tune, as a WAV file on a CD, was roughly ten times larger, far too big to readily share online back in those days. This slim file that could fit inside an e-mail, though? A game changer. As a computer programmer, Trieu instantly grasped what a huge deal it would become. Excited to share the discovery, Trieu e-mailed the MP3 to another friend, who wrote back, "Thanks. What is this file and how do I open it up?" He didn't have any software that could play it.

Lossy compression, used to create formats such as MP3s and online video, works by analyzing high-resolution files then trimming away the parts that humans don't pay too much attention to. You need sharp ears and good speakers to be able to distinguish between a song's full version and its lossy MP3 self. Other lossy digital audio compression formats exist, but MP3s are by far the most popular.

The scientists at Germany's Fraunhofer Institute who developed the MP3 algorithm utilized perceptual coding. Their software ranks all aspects of sound from "relevant" (to be compressed with maximum respect for fidelity) to "irrelevant" (to be relentlessly squashed; who's gonna notice?). The fuzzy science of psychoacoustics combines with automated value judgments. Welcome to the future, where humans teach machines to automatically strip information from art.

Comparison tests were necessary to fine-tune the algorithm, since different audio sources reacted to it in different ways. The task was to come up with a one-size-fits-all setting. Lead Fraunhofer engineer Karlheinz Brandenburg listened to Suzanne Vega's delicate a cappella "Tom's Diner" thousands of times, painstakingly adjusting the algorithm after each one in attempts to make the compressed version of her voice sound as naturalistic as the CD version. Since "Tom's Diner" was *only* a voice, the algorithm had no immediately "irrelevant" material to squish. Not only that: we're predisposed to extract all sorts of nuanced information from the human voice, so we notice when something is the slightest bit off. By honing in on acceptable settings for this particularly thorny case, Brandenburg did much to develop the overall aesthetic of MP3 compression. Hearing is believing, and what we're hearing is, in some small part, how Brandenburg wanted us to hear Vega.

When Suzanne Vega visited the Fraunhofer Institute years later, proud scientists played her the span of the "Tom's Diner" compression attempts. The crude early versions were "monstrous and weird," she wrote in an essay for *The New York Times*, "as though the *Exorcist* has somehow gotten into the system, shadowing every phrase." They concluded with the "clean" final version. Vega continued: " 'Actually, to my ears it sounds like there is a little more high end in the MP3 version? The MP3 doesn't sound as warm as the original, maybe a tiny bit of bottom end is lost?' I suggested. The man looked shocked. 'No, Miss Vega, it is exactly the same.'"

Bass, the lower frequencies associated with *the bottom* in all its ample meanings, so often turned up in Afro-diasporic music such as rap (German hip-hop was rising into mainstream popularity in those years), appeared to be lessened by the technocratic algorithm—according to the artist. A team of industry-approved experts overrode her individual experience. The woman's analysis was disregarded by the men. The psychoacoustic model created by Brandenburg and his team represents how they hear things; it is scientific but hardly objective. "Tom's Diner" reminds us that listening is always subjective, and that social prejudices in the tech milieu filter down into the code itself, even when the coders do not believe this to be possible.

What an MP3 is, for most of us, is *good enough*. Although perhaps their sheer ubiquity has trained us to agree with the software designers about what is sonically "irrelevant."

For a while, when someone asked what my favorite type of music was, I'd say 128 Kbps MP3s. And it was true! MP3s can be encoded at different resolutions, and Kbps refers to the amount of audio information (measured in kilobits) contained each second. At the high end, 320 Kbps MP3s sound virtually indistinguishable from the CD. A 128 Kbps MP3 takes up less space and is about as low as the fidelity can go before the audio starts to sound noticeably lessened, even when listened to through cheap earbuds. The balance of small file size with decent quality led audiobloggers to gravitate toward 128 Kbps MP3s. Perfect for online sharing, 128 Kbps MP3s widened the conversation. They let music move as nothing before had.

The psychoacoustic trickery of digital audio compression works wonders, but it should be done only once: squeezing down an already-compressed audio file—"transcoding"—generates unwanted digital errata called compression artifacts. It happens when you create an MP3 from an MP3, rip streaming audio, or upload MP3 audio to video-sharing sites. Transcoded audio sounds the way pixelated JPEGs and the blocky smudges in lo-res Web video look: grainy, smeary, imprecise. Bass tones hollow out. Detail in the upper registers, such as bright violin strings or sizzling hi-hat percussion, tarnishes.

Compression artifact crunchdown is the default setting for cheap or unlicensed digital content. This is the sound of files that have survived patchy connections and erroneous metadata, straddling pirate servers and shaky Bluetooth transfers and YouTube rips, evading spam filters en route to Russian warez sites to end up on a desktop or in some Web video accompanied by an equally messed-up JPEG. Transcoded audio serves as a pervasive reminder that the Web is not some frictionless information highway where everything is speedy and transparent—*Click Here to Learn More!*—but rather a superabundant and hopelessly cluttered digital warehouse distressed by user error, junk data, and bandwidth bottlenecks. *Click Here to Learn Less!* A compression artifacted patina tells us that the data has roamed far and wide, in and out of formats. In a very real sense compression *is* travel in a digital world.

THE CRAZIEST RIDDIM

Paid streaming services and legit MP3 stores maintain a transcode-free compression passageway from CD-quality audio to your ears. Taking it up a notch, HD video and hi-res audio require expensive systems of recording, editing, and playback to exist as such. Tidal offers lossless audio, for twice the going price of the regular stream subscription. This entertainment from on high is engineered to be read only. I find it untrustworthy, for it plumps and primes us to be an audience of consumers who should not speak back. So I embrace the transcodes. When media edits are hastily executed, unlicensed, or both, it's usually a sign that something interesting is bubbling up.

One winter, American producer Matt Shadetek was living in one of those East Berlin flats that you buy coal by the half ton to heat. In his morning routine he shoveled the stuff into the heater, prepped stovetop espresso, and sat down at his laptop to make beats while wearing a coat. After an hour or two of producing on one such day, he'd sketched out a short instrumental beat. An adrenaline-rush synthesizer line circled above ominous bass tones and a distorted kick drum. Twitchy hand claps jostled for space. It captured the pent-up energy of working in a freezing apartment while dreaming of dancing in a packed club. Like much of Shadetek's music, the song was inspired by U.K. grime, a hyperlocal London genre that drew on the city's rich legacy of rave and Caribbean sound-system culture, mixing it up with hungry MCs and video-game sonics.

The sketch was originally conceived as the intro to a mixtape. Later Matt slapped on a bootleg a cappella (he'd downloaded the MP3 from a pirate reggae site) and began to incorporate it into his DJ sets. Audiences reacted so well to its raw energy that Shadetek decided to flesh it out as a proper song with original vocals. A few months after its release, "Brooklyn Anthem (featuring 77Klash and Jahdan Blakkamoore)" got licensed for the *Madden NFL* video-game franchise.

What happened next happened quickly. *Madden* exposed Shadetek's song to gamers worldwide, but nowhere did it make more intuitive sense than in Brooklyn, home to one of the largest Caribbean communities outside the islands. Within a few days of the game's release, a local reggae crew called Island Superia Sounds had dug up the instrumental version of "Brooklyn Anthem" and given it the refix treatment. A refix is when you edit a song to emphasize some aspect of it while keeping the overall structure intact—not quite a remix. In this case, Island Superia chopped "Brooklyn Anthem" up just enough to be able to rebrand it as their own. Literally: none of the official voices remain; instead we hear someone shout "Island Superia Sound numba one!" Catchphrases from U.S. rapper Lil Jon and dancehall stars Elephant Man and Mavado splash across the track, to which they added vinyl backspins, sirens, and other sound effects in a successful bid to out-hype the original.

Island Superia included their refix on a promotional mix-tape handed out at SeaBreeze Manor, a tropical-themed club blessed by a homemade sound system in Bed-Stuy, where they hosted an all-ages party. Kids loved its anarchic vibe and pulse-quickening tempo. Island Superia's edit entered into heavy rotation as the moment to bust out your best dance moves. The refix exposed the song to a wider audience, in Brooklyn, than *Madden* had. Matt's cabin-fever-fueled dance track entered this new era of its existence rechristened the "Craziest Riddim."

Soon after, a skinny guy named Frosty Da Dancer was the first to upload cell-phone video footage of himself dancing to it. In the following weeks a hundred "Craziest Riddim" dance videos had leaped online. Kids shot themselves with cell phones or webcams, solo and in teams, dancing in backyards and on subway platforms, in bedrooms and Brooklyn streets. Some choreographies riffed off *The Matrix* riffing off Hong Kong kung fu flicks. Others drew inspiration from double-Dutch jump rope or contemporary dancehall fads. The most successful of the videos racked up more page views than the song's official video.

The videos also provided a platform for the dancers to experiment with the nonlinear edits of postproduction. The graceful kinetic energy captured by the camera is complemented by edit energy, with jump cuts from one location to another, text overlays, zoom and pans, bizarre filters, slo-mo, and more.

The "Craziest Riddim" dance videos, lo-res to begin with, are further compromised by the grainy pixelation of compression artifacts. And nobody cares. A strange freedom unfolds: as recording and playback devices (mostly phones) make lo-res (but fast-creation) tools widely available, the minimum production values needed to enter the global media game are lowered as well. Lossy compression is our gain.

Just a few years ago, a short film made with cheap equipment had no easy means of reaching viewers. Even if you sidestepped the gatekeepers, theaters and festivals demanded a modicum of quality: Could you project it on a screen? Was it TV-ready? These questions now seem strangely quaint. Shoot, edit, upload. The hard part is the dance.

Island Superia brought "Brooklyn Anthem" home. The original, made in Berlin, was about the borough. They set it in motion *in* the borough. Island Superia plucked it off corporate gaming platforms, modified its DNA, and planted those seeds in the youth-built, ad hoc network strung between dance videos and hype parties and Brooklyn's very real streets and subways.

The unpredictable path traveled by Shadetek's creation is a route that's going to be increasingly familiar as traditional notions of fidelity fall to the wayside in our on-demand, data-soaked world. More "connectivity" means the missed connections pile up faster too. Call it Babeltronics. Digital information zips around faster than its metadata, writing over any original context. The signal speeds into noise.

Matt didn't earn any money from the viral boost of "Brooklyn Anthem." The reward lay in the satisfaction of knowing that his song made its way back to the streets that inspired its creation, and in those travels was transformed into something that Brooklyn youth could call their own.

LISTENING, ROOTS, JAMAICA

When sounds travel faster than the speed of context, it can be useful to reexamine the roots, and what better place to get grounded than the small, philosophically minded Caribbean island where one city opened a portal into a world of dark-hearted, transcendent, shape-shifting sound? We're still walking through the gate they cleared, still figuring out what to do with all the space on the other side—the dub side. Where songs leave themselves to become something else.

Rhyming live over records. Subtracting elements from a completed song to make a ghostly new one. Studio engineer as creative artist. DJing as performance. Sound-system operators as hero-librarian-curators. It all sprang from Kingston, Jamaica. In the late sixties and seventies the capital city's music community developed and refined these techniques, and many more. Visionaries with names such as King Tubby and Lee "Scratch" Perry became our Plato and Socrates, laying down the foundations of contemporary electronic music culture. This is gospel to DJs and reggae fans. For the rest of us, the ideas they pioneered have become so embedded in mainstream musical thought as to nearly pass unperceived.

I knew all this when I first visited the island. It's well

documented, and yes, it's all there. The surprise, the thing that I couldn't have known until I went there, was how sound and community hunker down together for the long haul and thereby create the preconditions for all the remix/version migrations that we know the island for.

Right outside the music mecca of Kingston lies the modest town of Portmore. There, tucked behind a cluster of unpaved streets in the Gregory Park neighborhood, is an enormous metal gate with DI CONGOS H.Q. painted on it. For the last three decades, roots reggae group the Congos have been steadily building their physical and spiritual home here. What lies beyond this barrier is much more than a house with a music studio on a walled plot of land shaded by enormous trees. This is a Rasta place.

Rastafarianism is a low-fidelity religion, a belief system that's suspicious of the Bible's written word, in love with linguistic slippage, and unbelieving in any final say. The Rastas claim Ethiopia's autocratic emperor Haile Selassie as Christ, despite his protests otherwise, despite his death. Truth is a discourse. So they talk it out. Then talk some more.

Neighbors call the Congos' compound the lions' den. Friends drop by hoping to jam or simply share conversation over roast breadfruit or coconut or a spliff. Outside, acrid smoke rose lazily from a trash fire (garbage collection is nonexistent here), and extravagantly colored hummingbirds darted frenetically in the warm air. The Sunday-morning quiet was broken only by the tinny notes of "Fisherman," the Congos' most famous song, squeezed into a ringtone. Roydel Johnson, aka Ashanti Roy, a powerfully built, dreadlocked man in his late sixties, retrieved the phone from some hidden pocket and answered, "Fire burn!" Roy sat on a rough-hewn bench, directly across from a huge mural painted on the side of his house. It depicts the Last Supper, except Jesus Christ has been replaced by Haile Selassie dressed in full Ethiopian regalia, and there are thirteen disciples instead of twelve, among them Malcolm X, Paul Bogle, Bob Marley, two women, Roy, and his son. There's a Bible and a watermelon (partially eaten) and a bong, which, here, is called a chalice because herb is sacred and, before you smoke it, you should give thanks to Jah. When Lee Perry recorded the Congos on his Black Ark four-track back in 1977, producing their seminal record, *The Heart of the Congos*, he may have got that heart on tape, but its spirit is renewed daily among the people in this yard.

I was Ashanti Roy's houseguest a few days before the Christmas holiday, and while the goings-on in the yard were indeed amazing, I'd expected their epic levels of self-styled mythology and Rastafarian mysticism. The real eye-opener appeared quietly, as sounds floating over Roy's rear wall.

A neighbor was playing hip-hop. No big deal.

Then the more I listened, the more I realized just how much connoisseurship lay behind the selection. Singles from 2002, 2003. East Coast United States. Nearly entirely New York City rap. Not willfully obscure digger tunes, which I wouldn't have been able to ID, but a refined exploration of a specific moment. I love hearing good DJs wind their way through song selection, and this was an advanced take. It spoke to the power of thoughtful curation. An automated service could never come up with this type of playlist, linked as it was to an idiosyncratic appraisal of a specific era. I could appreciate the depths of it only because that early aughts moment coincided with my last years of weekly vinyl buying. The tunes brought back memories of late nights spent listening to rap radio in Brooklyn, weekly visits to Beat Street to check out the latest 12-inches, all the flavors of rap that fed its most devoted fans in that particular city in that particular moment. To stumble across a selection this focused, a decade after the fact, coming out from a tin-roofed lean-to in another country? Unheard of.

I never found out if it was the radio or a mixtape or whatever. I only knew it was the neighbors'. Wafting over the walls.

Two nights later I got woken up around 2:00 a.m. by a street party happening a few blocks away. In the middle of a set of good dancehall tunes, the DJ cut to George Michael's "Careless Whispers," spiked with laser sound F/X. It was the only British pop song I heard the entire night, and it was absurdly, jaw-droppingly right. Reggae purists exist—outside Jamaica. German, Italian, British, you name it. Inside Jamaica? Celine Dion is a virtual goddess. Michael Bolton headlines festivals. And although that night was ostensibly a dancehall party, the selector wanted George Michael and knew exactly when to drop it. Timing plus conviction is everything. The DJ transformed a song I'd heard countless times on easy-listening FM stations into a dancehall-smashing megaton bomb. It's not just that the music really is better in Kingston (although this is often the case), it's that one hears music one has already heard revitalized—made surprising again—in the best possible way.

Which, at 2:00 a.m. on Tuesday right before Christmas, was "Careless Whispers." With lasers.

The evening's other sound was dogs: a ragged chorus flared sporadically throughout the night. Not pets; protection. Neighborhood parties spread holiday cheer, but the looming elections kept everyone on edge. In Jamaica, both major political parties (the Jamaica Labour Party and the People's National Party) arm gangs, and those gangs clash. As this dance petered out, over in Spanish Town cops found Navardo Hodges of the Clansman gang with a bullet through his head—and the rest of his body a few blocks away. Violence in Jamaica crescendoed with the 2010 extradition to the United States of JLP-supporting gangsta boss Christopher "Dudus" Coke, and while the murder rate has gone down, it's still among the highest in the world.

Likkle David, the Congos' guitarist, discussed the brutal situation in Jamaica with me in his soft voice: "Music keep our mind from worrying about every problem. Music take us out of our environment. And [when] we do music, we see, we go in a different world in our mind. Even though we're right here. It's a form of transcendent feeling. To really stand in one place and jump up. You jump and you never move. You have to have imagination or you're nothing. You're hungry and you don't have nothing. And you can't find nothing. All you can find is this song, this sound inside of you. Before you know, you start to think about this sound, and then you forget about hungry. For a few hours, four, five, six, eight hours. And that just repeats itself until another day. And a lot of people survive like that for a while. Some don't."

Good music can stop time and blot out the pain. The heavier the workaday grind to escape from, the more a party transports us—provided you're really hearing the sound. Gravity and uplift. The harder you listen, the lighter you become.

I saw this casually serious approach to listening throughout Jamaica. I'd glimpse it while spinning around the radio dial or in little kids tunefully singing violent badman lyrics—you can't not pay attention to sound because it is ever present. Doesn't matter if you're in bed or skanking in front of the speaker stack at an impromptu street party: How can anyone fall asleep when the DJ's pacing and presentation is so thrilling? Life in this ultra-saturated music environment, where sound is publicly scruti-nized at every point of its existence, has many perks. The connoisseur listening audience drives musical evolution. De-mands it. This is the land of the soundclash, where multiple sound systems are set up in the same outdoor space to compete tune for tune. People vote with their feet; defeat is public. These intense feedback loops between audience and musician are the engine that sent the culture of remix and version worldwide.

Jamaica also has such brilliant audiences and listeners (and, yes, music) because of the relationship between class and noise. In urban spaces, the richer you are, the quieter it is where you live. In places such as the Congos' compound—open-air living in tropical climates, in densely populated neighborhoods—people aren't thinking, "We should be quiet for the sake of our neighbors," but rather, "We should select the best possible music at any given moment because our neighbors are gonna hear it." When you live without the means for much travel, it's best that you nurture the music you live with.

The Rae Town, Kingston, weekly street dance has been dedicated to oldies ever since it started back in 1982. Even around midnight, before things heated up, the Sunday-night scene was popping. Dapper grandparents dressed to the nines swayed to songs that were young when they were. Mohawked twentysomething ladies strutted fearlessly. "Yuh badda den dem?" a man with no prospects asked a two-hundred-pound woman in skintight clothes. "Yeah, I'm badda den dem!" Rudeboys on motorcycles preened up and down the street, until the crowd on either side of the road swelled into a single mass. Food vendors spread outward from the Capricorn Inn, the dance's epicenter, serving jerk chicken, fish tea, goatskin soup. They could raise their prices but don't, and this seems to be part of the Rae Town vibe. The audience is a respectful congregation, and the vendors' attitudes reflect that. Rae Town is Kingston's longest-running dance, and it is famously, specifically cool—cool like the Heptones sang "Cool Rasta" in '76, cool like the Wailers in their British TV debut on *Old Grey Whistle Test* back in '73.

The DJs revisited soul hits, songs that tend to populate the AM dial stateside. But here, everything was shifted. The main melody line sat in the background, the sweet vocals were in the middle, and right up front, rumbling the body, was the bass line's sturdy, propulsive bounce.

Hearing a recording you love played on a well-installed

sound system will take your breath away. Perhaps literally: when cranked up, systems such as the high-end club standard Funktion-One pump out sound with a ponderous physicality that can set your eyeballs shaking. As wonderful as they are, such systems tend to be clinical, a bit too crystal clear for my taste. You can tune a sound system for fidelity or personality. Rae Town goes for the latter. The Rae Town sound system was the loveliest I'd ever heard. Bass like a lover's embrace. As if to say, "This is how we do things here." The people have hand-built the sound system they're playing on. They've fine-tuned it over the years and can make adjustments on the fly if need be. The speakers pumping out oldies on a crowded street weren't loud; or rather, they were just loud enough to manifest the sound as a material medium enveloping the crowd. An ambient hug, unroofed audio rising on some gentle breeze. *And when we do music, we see*—imagine a flawless summer night or extra novocaine, weightlessness rocked by a tidal flow, the sonic equivalent of floating off a gorgeous Caribbean beach that you don't have to have money to stretch out on.

Street dances such as Rae Town are free, open to all. The idea of equality is so beautiful because it is so simple.

Rae Town lives by an ethos of localization. The dance has enlivened that corner for more than thirty years. Its vibe reaches across generations. The Sunday-night strip lights up into a community beacon, and a whole microeconomy piggybacks on that, with food sellers, walking vendors, and the like. Audio terroir. A sense of place articulated as sound, sound understood as a nurturing entity (Rae Town is basically dedicated to love songs)—all this was palpable.

To produce effective music with borrowed Jamaican voices is no major feat. Foreigners have a long and often acrimonious history of doing just that, but like newlyweds vacationing at Jamaica's all-inclusive, walled-off coastal resorts, it is a transaction that fails to enrich the community. Rae Town puts roots down. Music from Jamaica changed the world. Their studio innovations never cease to amaze. Yet this is a country that could never have invented headphones. The idea of having something clamped to your head, creating a private little soundworld for you alone? Nope. That wouldn't have flown at all. Headphones cut people off. It's a technology of isolation. The brilliance of Jamaican music lives for and in the public.

At their best moments, music and community blend into one living thing. Every participant becomes a caretaker. This is why a guitar leans against the holy table in the Congos' Last Supper mural. This is what admiring Japanese nerds wandering around Rae Town know. In the record shops dotting Tokyo's Shinjuku, one can find all this music alphabetized into neat little racks. It's *much* easier to buy Jamaican music in Japan than in Jamaica: more choice, better organization. But you can't buy or sell the thing that makes it come alive. This is something inborn. It happens only here.

Back in home in New York City, I walked into an art supply shop near the School of Visual Arts in Manhattan. They were playing an ace selection of Jamaican rocksteady from the 1960s. I told the clerk at the cash register how much I liked the music, then asked him what it was. "Oh"—he shrugged—"it's Spotify."

It didn't occur to him to mention the name of the currently playing song, or the artist performing it, or even the name of whatever Spotify channel it was. The important thing, the identifying bit of info, to him, was Spotify. After Jamaica, this felt like a slap in the face.

All that is solid melts into cloud-based streaming platforms.

I love listening to radio not knowing what I'm hearing. I've lost afternoons to hearing a gorgeous unfamiliar melody, then following it for as long as I could.

On some level, the clerk listening to Jamaican gold and not caring what he was listening to was fine, or at least unavoidable. Ignorance is a by-product of what happens when sounds travel. Music's ability to surprise is a large part of its magic for many, and surprise and ignorance dance hand in hand. The difference between them is that surprise entails going toward the thing that you do not yet know, and ignorance involves stepping away from it. Put another way, George Michael occupying pride of place at peak time in a dancehall set and every other so-wrong-it's-right selection is that difference. Asking about a song and getting to speak with strangers about something they're passionate about is that difference.

I said thanks and walked out.

AFRICAN DISTORTIONS

The ungraspable swirl of digital flotsam hinders our ability to locate ourselves, just as surely as deeply rooted places such as

Kingston leverage that grounding to send musical ideas around the world. These two conditions come to a head in the strange story of a band that didn't change their music or location for three decades, then suddenly shot into international notoriety.

In 1987, the year of their debut LP, the Western world just wasn't ready for the music of L'Orchestre Folklorique Tout Puissant Likembé Konono N°1—or Konono, for short. The scrappy Congolese folk outfit had been around since the late sixties, a rotating ensemble of nearly a dozen singers, dancers, percussionists, and likembé thumb piano players who came together to perform traditional West African regional songs—but with a twist. Their acoustic instruments couldn't compete with the urban roar of the Congo's capital city, Kinshasa, so they decided to fight volume with volume. Even the most basic audio gear was hard to come by—Congo was in the midst of a long-simmering war for independence—so Konono improvised: they fashioned crude microphones from abandoned car-alternator magnets; they beefed up their rhythm section with pots, pans, and whatever piece of scrap metal was lying around; and they blasted their live performances through industrial loudspeakers salvaged from the police headquarters of the country's former Belgian rulers. If nothing else (besides ear-shattering volume), their resulting sound had buzz.

In fact, loud buzzing music was not without precedent in Western Africa. For centuries mild distortion performed an intimate, spiritual role in regional thumb-piano music. Folk tradition maintained that rattle and buzz attracted ancestors' spirits, so seashells (or, more recently, bottle caps) were affixed to the metallic thumb pianos. The pianos' gently percussive, melodic notes were played for the enjoyment of the living; the resonant buzz and overtones of the seashells and bottle caps reverberated with the spirit world. In the early sixties Konono unwittingly took this heaven-and-earth aesthetic to the extreme: amid the clamor of downtown Kinshasa, their performances were so buzzingly loud and distorted that they probably drew a small army of curious ancestral spirits.

In the fullness of time Konono would attract devoted troops of fans among the living—but that was not for thirty years to come. For the first three decades of their existence Konono N°1 was obscure even in their hometown; they played hotels, weddings, funerals, and street corners. Even at the weirdest moments of their performances, Konono's muscular, infectious sound stemmed from the rich musical talents that led to Congolese bands dominating African charts for much of the twentieth century. Ethiopia was long known for its suave, vibraphone-heavy jazz; Fela Kuti put Nigeria on the musical map with his politically charged Afrobeat funk. But the music of Congo was always festive—and a Konono show would often feel like an especially rowdy party teetering on the brink of chaos. Their basic live setup stayed pretty much the same over the years: a trio of younger men created complex, polyrhythmic grooves by layering and looping (and amplifying) simple melodies plucked off on their thumb pianos. Female dancers would weave through a cluster of percussionists who were beating the life out of their homemade drums. Vocalists would work their way to the front of the stage

and occasionally tell light moral tales, but mostly opt for joyful
shouts of audience exhortation. The linchpin of the whole ensemble was Le President, an elderly man in a dapper three-
piece suit, sitting at the center in a folding lawn chair,
detachedly observing the crowd as his band whipped them
into a frenzy.

Despite the talent and energy of its central players, Konono's
shambolic carnival clatter was generally considered hick music
by the locals. Kinshasa saw plenty of urbane, outward-looking
local bands who yearned for wider success—the sort of aspiring
young stars who dressed sharp and kept their eyes glued to MTV
Africa. Compared to them, Konono's country-bumpkin aesthetic was almost embarrassing. Their old instruments and jerry-
rigged gear spoke to no aspirations for fame and fortune.

In 1987, a state-owned French ethnographic record label heard
good things about Konono and released a twenty-six-minute
song of theirs on a small-run compilation LP: *Musiques Urbaines à Kinshasa*. The album reached only the most devoted
African-music aficionados—and even they were mostly turned
off by its bruised rumble. *Musiques Urbaines* got virtually no
attention and quickly lapsed into obscurity. Konono returned
to their day jobs and gigs at hotel bars for another fifteen years.

Fast-forward to 2004. Thanks to music blogs and fledgling
file-sharing sites such as Napster, the record stores' outdated
organizational logic was beginning to crumble into the beauti-
fully messy sprawl of online musical fandom. It was no longer
strictly Rock in one bin, World Music in another. The canonical

gatekeepers of World Music were officially bypassed when some die-hard Konono fan digitized one of the original copies of *Musiques Urbaines à Kinshasa* and uploaded the MP3s to a music file-sharing site. Konono began to make the rounds on the Internet. Something about their sound—distorted, homespun, libidinous, rhythmically complex—caught the ears of hungry young music fans in North America and Europe. As much as Konono's sound signified "antique African," something about it was also undeniably punk rock—an echo of the loud, saw-toothed dissonance of early Sonic Youth, or the sweaty, over-driven experimental noise rock that was sweeping college radio and underground music venues throughout the western hemisphere.

In one of history's ironies, the Congo was home to gifted guitarist and bandleader Franco Luambo Makiadi. He released more than 150 records, and in recent years reissues have hit the World Music scene. Many consider Franco to be the first African musician—i.e., the first musician to achieve international popularity and influence across the continent. Yet it was Konono's amped-up thumb pianos that won the attention of guitar-loving indie rockers across the States and Europe.

In 2003 an enterprising Belgian promoter brought Konono to Europe, pairing them with postpunk icons the Ex, whose music brought noise, folk, and improv into the same rhythmically charged space. None of Konono's dozen members had ever before left Africa. But no matter—they absolutely killed it, night after night. Konono's raucous, earsplitting live shows enthralled audiences. Terrie Hessels, one of the Ex's guitarists, released their debut CD, a live recording of their first gig on that auspicious tour. By then, the Belgian label Crammed had caught wind of Konono and signed them up for a series of new releases. *Congotronics*, their first studio album, was an overnight online hit. Their photogenic lo-fi approach was candy to the Western press. Aided by shrewd marketing and a heavy dose of sonic distortion, the music won over African-roots fans, experimental-electronica kids, and punk rockers. NPR ate them up. *Congotronics* appeared on everyone's annual top-ten lists. World Music finally got hip.

Konono N°1 has since graced the cover of the vaunted British music magazine *The Wire*, played Central Park Summerstage, toured alongside Björk, and written a song with jazz legend Herbie Hancock. They received a pair of Grammy nominations. These examples are just some of the bewildering, improbable events that were set into motion when an aging, illiterate, down-and-out hotel band from war-torn Africa suddenly became avatars of indie cool. Locals in their hometown refer to all this, with ominous awe, as the Konono Case.

In recent years variations on the Konono Case—when a local group leapfrogs over any peer approval to sell out concerts several thousand miles away—have proliferated. Closest to home, Crammed started promoting Staff Benda Bilili, another photo-ready Congolese band with a too-good-to-be-true backstory. The group consists of four polio-crippled men who maneuver in homemade tricycle rigs, accompanied by a teenage boy who plays an instrument he fashioned from a tin can and a single guitar string. When Staff Benda Bilili are not performing to rave reviews in Europe ("They were, without qualification or allowance, the most exciting band to emerge from Africa in years . . . Very, very strong. Very, very great. Very, very loud" ran a typical review, in the *Financial Times*), the homeless band squat in and around the ramshackle Kinshasa zoo.

Another Konono Case is Syrian wedding singer Omar Souleyman. He was virtually unknown until Sublime Frequencies, a label run by a freaky art-rock collective in Seattle, heard a Souleyman cassette while on vacation in Syria and began reissuing his music on CD. Now he's firmly established on the international tour circuit that Konono N°1 opened up. Central Park Summerstage, a Björk collaboration, the European festival rounds? Like Konono, Souleyman's now done that too.

Unlike Konono's repertoire, which even folks in Kinshasa regarded as oddball, Souleyman's genre, *dabke*, enjoys incredible popularity across the Levant and in immigrant spaces such as Brooklyn's Bay Ridge, home to several active bands. None of the actual *dabke* fans I've met have had any idea who Omar Souleyman is. And why should they? Other artists in the genre do more interesting work. (I'm particularly fond of a strain featuring fifteen-minute songs constructed around dubbed-out flute riffs.)

The most newsworthy aspect of Omar Souleyman is how successfully he has been marketed to a Western audience. Ever since he broke in the West, Souleyman hasn't needed the appreciation of people who can understand what he's singing. Despite the flavor of open-mindedness surrounding it, Souleyman's popularity in the West relies on a larger incuriosity—a lack of basic engagement with Levantine culture. Ignorance of *dabke* is a prerequisite for his success. To respect *dabke* as an active, lived music scene would require acknowledging that Souleyman is eclipsed by many other more creative, more influential *dabke* artists. Plucking an artist from a scene and repackaging him or her for wider consumption is as old as the music biz itself, but that doesn't make it any less annoying. I've yet to see a review of Souleyman's work that mentions any other *dabke* performers. When music marketing reinforces cultural distance and closes the door on musical understanding, everybody gets shortchanged.

Will we in the West ever really know what Konono N°1 was about? Does it matter? The musicians of Konono had lyrics, dances, histories for their music; we heard Africans who kinda sounded like experimental-rock jam bands from Brooklyn. The matter wasn't helped by Konono's Belgian label's never bothering to print any lyrics. Back in 1987 the liner notes of the French ethnographic LP laid the groundwork for further exoticization: "The band, of Angolan origin, plays authentic folklore from Angola from such places as Zaka-Zaka. Nzu-Nlaza, the leader of the band, has no hesitation in disciplining its members when they become unruly . . . The main concern of the band being to blast out the sound as loud as possible, they play in front of a wall of six speakers, only three of which contain loudspeakers."

I know that Africans and blacks have been fetishized for centuries now, perhaps millennia. Who cares? You simply exist in all your complexity and let them deal with it. Fetishism is so vague. I care a lot when Westerners rip off non-Western musicians, even by rendering them anonymous as Sublime Frequencies often did, but random concepts of fetishization don't mean much. It's almost too abstract to matter.

Musicians like getting paid to play, they like getting credited for their work, and if they're singing or rapping, they want you listen to their words. It's that simple. The Konono Case is an awesome thing if it means, say, more African bands can travel and make a living outside their home countries.

At the end of their first European tour, nine members of Konono—two-thirds of the band—chose to remain in Europe, likely by paying fees or service to the Belgian Mafia or their Congolese partners. To their tour manager's horror, only three members were present by the time of their final concert, in Amsterdam's respected Paradiso venue. The rest had slipped away into a shadowy underworld.

I tried without success to track down the original touring crew. No dice: their story is literally off-the-record. But it's a familiar one, repeated among millions of undocumented people.

The first musician I befriended in Madrid shared this commonplace story. I was living in a month-to-month aparthotel for the summer. It's never clear exactly who ends up in places like that, but there I was, suffering through the roach infestation and the lousy microkitchen and the nosy, work-allergic doorman. One day the unit next to mine was blasting Deep Forest, the Grammy-winning faux-ethnic ambient pop manufactured by two Frenchmen. The next day the same apartment was playing Fantômas, a cinematic experimental-metal project by Faith No More front man Mike Patton. I had to find out what sort of person would go from ambient cheese to avant-garde mayhem. So I met Mark, a wiry black African with dreadlocks and a music collection whose organizational logic left me baffled. We spoke in Spanglish. Mark was never precise about his past (or his present). He was a percussionist. He looked ten years older than me. So far as I could tell, a fully electronic drum kit was his only possession of value, apart from some scattered items of clothing (and the inexplicable CD collection).

We drifted together that summer, then apart. Walking down a Barcelona street at 3:00 a.m. two years later, we bumped into each other; I was moving to Barcelona, he was already there. Later we discovered that we were living kitty-corner from each other in La Barceloneta, a peninsular speck of land by the beach that once housed Andalusian fishermen. La Barceloneta's beach-facing boardwalks were thick with international tourists, but the musty inner streets were for the working poor (those same international tourists had started buying up property there but didn't yet have a presence). Mark was sick, squatting in his ex's apartment, one hundred meters from the Mediterranean. He had to sneak in and out and couldn't use electric lights after dark for fear of alerting others to his presence. He hadn't set foot on the beach in months. Direct sunlight only reaches the narrow streets of the Barceloneta at midday. Whether it's migrants crossing the straits or people living under dark pressures so close to the expansive sea, the Mediterranean Gothic is real.

Bit by bit Mark's story emerged. He'd been an army musician, good enough to join his home country's international showcase band. Mark had always dreamed of going to New York to make it big, so when the troupe performed in southern Spain near the end of a long tour, he decided to stay. Europe first, then maybe, eventually, America. Mark started walking and didn't stop for a long time. A walk longer than you'll ever have to take, if you are lucky. By the end he'd become both a deserter and an illegal immigrant.

All the world's a stage when you're on tour, or at least that's what it feels like for every musician, each night a new city where you step into the spotlights. You've been invited. To hold the room's attention in your palm and show the people gathered as much beauty in the strength of your story-in-sound as they can apprehend.

But for those from unpopular countries who try to remain in a country that wants them as temporary entertainers but not permanent residents? The day after the gig you wake up and stroll out into something like shadows. The tales of people who turn their back on one country to disappear into another are blank, short little stories. From making records to going off-record. Names changed to protect the innocent. And yet for every musician who disappears, it seems that anonymity in Europe or America beats the occasional bursts of stardom onstage.

And that's the silence after the song.

4

WORLD MUSIC 2.0

Lasers in the jungle somewhere
Staccato signals of constant information
—PAUL SIMON, "The Boy in the Bubble"

In 1986, Paul Simon released *Graceland*, a pop album recorded in apartheid-era Johannesburg featuring Zulu a cappella singing and South African township jazz. The album skyrocketed to number one, went quintuple platinum, and helped usher African pop into mainstream visibility. Less than a year later, a group of industry bigwigs were sitting around a conference table in London, discussing how best to cash in on this newfound public interest in non-Western music. "The main problem in selling our kind of material," ran the meeting notes, "lay with the U.K. retail outlets and specifically the fact that they did not know how to rack it coherently." In other words, there was no shortage of albums that fit the bill; sellers simply needed a catchall term—a store "rack" name—to steer prospective buyers toward this wealth of music from hundreds of different countries, languages, traditions, from around the globe. *Hot* and *Tropical* were among the candidates discussed, but *World Music* won the day.

From the start, World Music was a promotional catchphrase, a commercial attitude rather than an audio descriptor, however vague, such as rhythm and blues. It remains a top-down affair. Managers groom bands, publicists chaperone album reception, booking agents handle live appearances. World Music is nothing if not professional, as reflected in its steep ticket prices and predilection for institutional venues subsidized by taxpayer dollars. The audience tends toward thirtysomethings and up, those who can afford to pay a little extra for a cultural adventure, the exotic made accessible.

World Music fandom drew on a handful of precedents: the mystic overtones that led the Beatles and their teeming admirers to embrace Ravi Shankar's sitar playing in the 1960s; the sober ethnographic field-recording LPs from Smithsonian Folkways, which took pains to present unadulterated cultural vistas; well-marketed stereotypes of the carefree, rootsy African musicians and freedom-loving reggae singers such as Bob Marley (World Music shied away from the increasingly political tenor of black American music in the 1970s); "Egyptian" belly-dance albums whose primary appeal was probably the busty models in orientalist lingerie on the covers rather than the saccharine music played by unenthusiastic Armenian American studio musicians.

Given how corny World Music was at the time, I'm lucky that I got into foreign sounds at all.

It was exactly the thing that fifteen-year-olds aren't supposed to hear: *Eat Shit Noise Music*. Late-night college radio had introduced me to Japan's virtuoso bass and drums duo, Ruins, and my quest for material by the spastic, proggy group was sending me down increasingly unusual paths. *Eat Shit* was my best lead—a bootleg cassette of Japanese groups available via RRRecords' mail-order catalog. Ruins were on the tracklist and the price was cheap.

RRRecords, a store dedicated to extreme music, was located, improbably, in the nearby mill town of Lowell, Massachusetts, where it served as a key node in the experimental-cassette circuit that flourished in the 1980s and early '90s. Digging through Boston's secondhand record shops one day I'd found a photocopied RRR catalog on the floor. The Ruins were the only artist names I recognized, and that chance occurrence expanded my ideas of what was possible in music. Prior to the Internet, grassroots noise culture was international by necessity—there simply weren't enough fans in any one place. So it was held together by slow postal services and scrawled addresses, mail order and tiny labels and kids swapping tapes. A good zine was gold.

The cassette arrived suspiciously fast, just two days after I'd posted my check. I tore open the package, armed my tape deck, and cranked the volume. What I heard became my personal ground zero. Dynamic, lascivious violence poured from the speakers, courtesy of Yamatsuka Eye's pre-Boredoms outfit, Hanatarash. Simultaneously atrocious and amazing, the sounds defied me not to like them, yet somehow I did, turned on by flashes of anarchic joy amid the audio fallout. I think I may have blushed. It wasn't that Hanatarash were throwing music rule books in the trash—that would have been relatively simple, or at least recognizable. No, their opening track sounded like rabid forces tearing down a house, or attempting to build one with cracked power tools and constantly splintering lumber. Somebody had a heavy thumb on the pause button, for the song would periodically shudder, accelerate, or drop out entirely. Not even the mic was exempt from abuse. Intermittent howls from Eye accompanied the bedlam. My teen mind melted.

I listened to *Eat Shit* over and over, extracting more meaningful signals from that noise than an optimistic chaos theorist would have thought possible. Other material on the comp was informed by a rampaging beat or sludge-filled guitar, always with screams, abject electronics, and/or feral distortion. But Hanatarash's three contributions were constructed from excitingly literal, nonmusical sounds lacking identifiable referent. Somebody's hitting ... something. As something else collapses. Titles such as "Frog Girl 90000" and "My Dad Is Car" offered little insight beyond "English as a second language" allusions to mechanized and mutated humans.

Cryptic and deranged, yes. But also strikingly earnest. The anarchic, excrement-fixated music spawned a strangely demotic threshold for its enjoyment: either you like this shit or you don't. There wasn't much room for debate. Issues of quality, musicianship, fidelity, funkiness, lyrical content, rhythmic prowess, historical relevance, etc., had no business here. This was stuff so

ugly only a mother or close relative could love it, and thus I
quickly found myself in the family.

For this was the first music that I could call my own. Reaching literally across the globe, the most unmarketable sounds
had located the right ears and transmuted into personal trea-
sure. Nobody was telling me how to listen or what to listen for.
I had discovered it unaided by recommendation, radio play, or a
journalist's review. *Eat Shit* slipped into my system like a car-
jacker, and the shock was total. My response was to make it
mine, to approach the music on its own terms while fashioning
my own yardstick for its enjoyment. Under the noise's surface
outrage lay a gambit for freedom.

The RRR cassette was polarizing, but it was also fragile,
personal even; and I had the sense that if I didn't listen closely, it
might pass unnoticed. I knew nothing about these groups, but an
individual with access to a photocopier and dual cassette deck
could obviously make a substantial difference in their world.
This scene had a tangible scale. It stood within grasp, which
suggested that I could actively participate in music—any music,
especially the weird stuff—rather than remain a well-informed
consumer. Precisely the sort of thing a resourceful kid in
New England's whitewashed cultural landscape needs to hear.

The casual listener might call the music on *Eat Shit* repellent. The refined listener might too. I thought of its force as
centrifugal, pulling us toward uncharted perimeters and away
from any stabilizing center.

Hitting these extremities at such a young age meant that
everything else in my record collection—dancehall reggae,

Mission of Burma, Detroit techno, Pere Ubu—got nudged a bit closer to the middle. They weren't well-known, but at least those cats had decent distribution! I grew curious. What other sounds lived in the undergrowth, off the map, in places you need an obscure catalog to locate?

Japanese noise taught me that experiencing the world via music or travel is *supposed* to be strange. Acknowledging that you don't know what's going on while being willing to linger, listen, and learn is all it takes. Noise appreciated as poetry becomes music. Foreign languages learned turn familiar. Allegedly exotic sounds approached on their own terms—whether it's sacred music from a Vietnamese temple or Hanatarash's calamity waltz—can reemerge as soul and set up camp inside yours.

A year after my Japanese noise epiphany I came across a seven-minute jam by a Marrakech Gnawa troupe that kickstarted my lifelong love affair with Moroccan music. It was compiled on a CD of fusion-minded World Music, yet the song was thankfully presented as is, without the meddling saxophones or ambient synth overdubs that marred the rest of the album. Gnawa is wonderful stuff. Plaintive call-and-response vocals sung in Arabic accompany a swirling clatter of hand claps and metal percussion. Bass lines reminiscent of roots reggae tie the whole thing together. It felt simple—familiar even—until I tried to anticipate when the bass melody would repeat, or when the vocals might enter or exit, and realized that I couldn't.

Everything clicked into place when I learned that Gnawa was the music of sub-Saharan Africans who'd been enslaved

and taken up into North Africa. As an Afro-Arab hybrid
with a distinct root in slavery's displacements, Gnawa spoke to
the ways black struggle found freedom and form in music. The
subtle, supple sense of time was one aspect of it. Gnawa cere-
monies, I read in the liner notes, can last for hours and are said
to be able to cure snakebites or usher bad vibrations from a
new house. From fascinating historical backstory to those cap-
tivating bass lines, I embraced it as I did the Japanese noise:
this was *my* music. The esoteric Afro-Sufi culture of Gnawa
was an ocean away, but the music it produced? That I could
dive into.

From then on, I sought out Maghrebi music like a fiend.
The more I looked, the more I found, an inexhaustible tumble
of styles that rewarded my curiosity at every turn. How could
one place produce everything from exuberant techno in the
Rif mountains to elegant old Spanish-Jewish-Arabic Andalusian songs? As I learned more about what was popular in the
country, it slowly dawned on me that the music that got lauded
within Morocco had virtually no overlap with the stuff successfully presented outside its borders. Even my beloved Gnawa led
a touristic existence within Morocco. It was a fascinating, troubling disjunction.

The most outrageous case of this is downright surreal. The
Rolling Stones guitarist Brian Jones produced an album of
Berber *taktouka jabalia* (mountain drums) in 1971. The group
he recorded, the Master Musicians of Jajouka, has enjoyed inter-
national cult status ever since. Famous Westerners pilgrimaged to
Jajouka to listen or jam along: Beat godfather William Burroughs,

jazz legend Ornette Coleman (whose wailing horns made for an easy fit), Mick Jagger (with video crew), Billy Corgan of the Smashing Pumpkins, Sonic Youth guitarist Lee Ranaldo, and . . . you get the point. Philip Glass produced the reissue of *Brian Jones Presents the Pipes of Pan at Joujouka*. Despite this acclaim, the Master Musicians are unknown a few towns over. American percussionist Grey Filastine visited Jajouka in the mid-nineties to meet the band and study their rhythms. Afterward, he traveled around northwestern Morocco. "Every time I went to a tape stall in the Rif region," Grey told me, "I would ask for *taktouka jabalia* and get cassettes of other groups, wearing similar clothes, playing the same instruments, and even many of the same melodies. But I couldn't find Jajouka for sale."

Jajouka's international cool cred led to a strange problem, one enabled and exacerbated by the music's local obscurity. For most of the last decade, two bands from Jajouka—a village with approximately six hundred inhabitants—have both claimed to be the Master Musicians. They are differentiated by a single transliteration choice. It's the Master Musicians of *Joujouka* versus the Master Musicians of *Jajouka*. Each band lists the Brian Jones album and an eponymous 1973–74 release in its discography. Each claims *they* collaborated with Ornette Coleman and Bill Laswell. Each band's website displays a scanned document from William Burroughs, and each cites it as evidence of their authenticity. (Heroin addict, wife killer, trust-funded avant-gardist: Burroughs was an unlikely candidate to settle disputes over musical stewardship in rural Africa.)

The argument over the "true" Master Musicians only matters because so much money rides on it. Western music industry royalties and concert fees can go a long way in the Rif. Audiences want the real thing, not ersatz imitators or greedy splinter groups. In an era when international pop stars are manufactured by image consultants and viral marketing campaigns, genuinely representative bodies from far-flung locales are more in demand on the World Music circuit than ever before.

Brian Jones recorded Jajouka more than forty years ago—clearly neither of today's Master Musicians retains any singular essence from that lineup. There is no essence; the Master Musicians' unusual debate is at odds with the Jajouka musical tradition, in which songs are learned over years, in communal lessons woven into the fabric of daily existence. One of the defining aspects of folk music is openness: if you can play it, it's yours. Like speaking a language, the ability to perform unwritten music confers—*is*—its own legitimacy. Both Master Musicians share a repertoire with each other and with other local bands. This genre of *taktouka jabalia* rings out across the Rif and around the world, multiplying without consensus, accompanied by acrid online battles, disputed *Wikipedia* entries, contentious open letters, and sporadic protests outside concerts. The wealth of music from this tiny section of North Africa has enough power to fuel much rejoicing and debate for years to come.

I'd incorrectly assumed that World Music was the process by which relevant regional talents got repackaged and sold to a Western audience. The Moroccan situation showed me that

that wasn't always the case. A British rock star can stumble into one village among thousands and have his presence authenticate the music there for the outside world. Authenticity plus star association: the mix is so valuable that infighting continues to this day.

Yes, World Music middlemen often help superstars such as Senegal's honey-voiced Youssou N'Dour and Algeria's charismatic raï crooner Khaled rise from national fame to international acclaim. But the lazy or downright bad World Music hustlers cherry-pick or even create acts guided not by any notion of quality that the band and their fans believe in, but rather based on what sound and story line is most appealing to an audience not remotely interested in learning about other cultures much less challenging their notion of the exotic (see the Putumayo label, whose motto is "Guaranteed to make you feel good!"). This sort of commercially minded sloppiness reinforces stereotypes.

A few years ago I visited the World Music industry in its natural habitat. After years spent in independent music circles, what could be more exotic than a roomful of people making money off music from countries they'll never visit, sung in languages they'll never learn? I'm talking about WOMEX—the World Music Expo, the Coachella of the World Music professional set.

I'd been invited to perform in Copenhagen, Denmark, where WOMEX was that year (it shifts locations throughout Europe). The lineup was epic: five days, a hundred bands from almost every country. Ten thousand publicists, booking agents, managers, label bosses, festival programmers, tourism-board delegations, cultural attachés, event producers, and a few hard-core fans came together to network, schmooze, get an ear on the hotly tipped sounds, and, if lucky, cut a few deals. They call themselves Womexicans. The daytime activity at WOMEX oscillates between promotional booths and panels with topics such as "Successfully Tapping into the Online and Mobile Revenue Stream: The Situation with Niche World Music." This gives way to evening music showcases. Bands performing there are paid less than at similar commercial events because doing so is seen primarily as an investment, a catalyst that will lead to greater economic opportunities. A particular buzz was in the air that year. Crammed Discs won the WOMEX Top Label Award, and the paraplegic, zoo-squatting Congolese musicians of Staff Benda Bilili, Crammed's heavily promoted band, landed the WOMEX Artist Award. The whole experience opened my eyes, but one concert in particular summed up many of World Music's quirks and limitations.

"This next band is called Yilila. They're supposed to be color-ful," said my friend from Ethiopia as he took the final drag from his cigarette. Four white guys in jeans and button-up shirts strolled onto the stage. One was set up at an Indian tabla, another perched behind a rock drum kit; the other two rounded it out on keyboards and bass. They played about five minutes of atmo-spheric light rock. Promotional materials explained that Yilila "come from one of Australia's most remote Aboriginal commu-nities." This was not adding up. These guys looked like accoun-tants. Synthesizer washes flowed past the pitched percussion of the Indian tabla. "I'm not seeing any color," I said. The white dudes grooved on. My African friend peered more closely at his concert guide.

Suddenly, as if on cue, the color arrived: two aborigines crept out of smoke-machine fog, wearing only bright red loincloths, complicated headbands, and lots of white body paint. They were wielding didgeridoos, as mesmerizing an icon of World Music as the tabla. A third aborigine took vocal duties; he wore jeans and a red shirt. After another song or two, one of the white players told the audience that this music was "traditional." These guys, he explained, were Australian natives and had been doing this type of music and dance for hundreds, or thousands—or was it tens of thousands?—of years. You don't need to be so precise with mythic time.

An Indian American woman who managed some African hip-hop acts stood at my side and asked, "What do you think?" Their concert presentation left me with the distinct sensation that it had come into being not out of any artistic or creative impulse, but rather to fulfill an economic role: to play at festivals in Australia (and, ideally, beyond) where white-aborigine cultural collaboration has value. The music was anodyne, but what really rubbed me the wrong way was how the band had assigned duties. The white guys got to wear Western casual. The aborigines? They had thongs and face paint (and little else). The onus of authenticity, so important to World Music audience-performer dynamics, lay on them. The brown guys. Demonstrating one's authenticity is work, after all, so this division of labor struck me as lopsided, especially considering that their music was based on a fusion approach where mix-and-match was king. Why didn't the visuals reflect that?

"Maybe I'd like them more if the white men were wearing the red thongs and body paint, and the black guys had on jeans and tucked-in polos," I said to her. After another song or two, I left Yilila to their soft rock–didgeridoo fusion and strolled outside to watch my friend smoke another cigarette. Imagine if one of the shirtless, pantless aborigines had spoken to the audience between songs instead? "Our white handlers have been performing their managerial duties for decades . . . centuries now. This is a traditional Australian cultural arrangement . . ." Would I have been the only one applauding?

World Music festivals will pay good cash for groups from "remote" places whose presence reinforces the idea that our planet is still filled with the kind of mystery that allows indigenous traditions to continue without interference from cell phones or multinational corporations. Especially in Europe, where such concerts are both plentiful and well funded. In regions where traditional music is actually traditional (read: ignored by the younger generation and/or performed solely for tourists), usually little money is to be had otherwise. So you take off your sneakers and shirt and put on the face paint.

So what about my failed joke—the concept, the possibility, of a thong swap? Races trade outfits while everything else remains the same: the music, the media-primed biography, the histrionic dancing, the dude rocking a tabla, the spectacle of a so-called ancient culture onstage with none of the historical texture that might make it relevant to us mangy internationals, gathered together in the world's most expensive concert hall. People would be confused, vaguely insulted, a tang of cynical satire would be in the air: "Why are they wearing that ridiculous face paint? This isn't Australian . . ." Jeans and casual dress shirts as camouflage, as twenty-first-century masks.

#WEARETHEWORLD

The last aboriginal music I'd heard prior to Yilila was Wilcannia Mob, a preteen hip-hop crew whose demo got pressed into my hands on my first Australian tour. On "Down River" endearingly mundane outback raps flowed over a didgeridoo-beatbox rhythm. "When the river's high we jump off the bridge / And when we get home we play some didge." It was actually pretty good. The cut-up didgeridoo sample tapped into the aboriginal instrument's throaty roar without making it seem folkloric the way Yilila and many other New Agers had.

Four years after my WOMEX experience, I was walking around sticky summertime Brooklyn, giving an eager first listen to M.I.A.'s second album, *Kala*. Midway through, a familiar tune came on. It took me a few seconds to recognize "Down River," unchanged except for guest verses from M.I.A. A song that was virtually unknown outside its home country ended up on a U.S. major label, repackaged as M.I.A.'s "Mango Pickle Down River featuring Wilcannia Mob." If Yilila and WOMEX

are consummate World Music entities, Wilcannia Mob—
aboriginal hip-hoppers whose work got versioned by a cosmopolitan tastemaker—embody what I like to call World Music
2.0. (Some refer to the phenomenon as global ghettotech,
tropical bass, global bass, or similar. Others, preferring taxon-
omy, list specific microgenres instead, coining neologisms when
necessary.)

Whereas World Music began life as a marketing term
handed down to the masses from an industry cabal, World
Music 2.0 sprouted up in the networked spaces of the Web.
In sharp contrast to its predecessor, World Music 2.0 is an anarchic young mess. A bottom-feeder, in the last decade it has
arisen from microcultures breeding on YouTube, invite-only
chat rooms, and other obscure corners of the Internet where
the line between producer and consumer blurs, and most
songs end up being given away for free. It is a music of mayfly
styles, porous sensibilities, and software sound presets. World
Music 2.0 begins before the band, even before the songs, starting off with DJ remixes or lo-fi party footage videos. Some of it
is not so great, but quite a lot is amazing, a jambalaya of sounds
that would have been unimaginable a few years ago.

Burn that guitar. Axe the Steinway. World Music 2.0 reflects that the computer is now the most common instrument.
As a result, age-old prerequisites for music-making no longer
apply. A physical instrument and space to practice it without
disturbing your family or neighbors? No longer needed. Dex-
terity, technique, muscle memory? Out the window. The only

requirement is computer access, although in a pinch, a PlayStation or smartphone will do.

I've always maintained that World Music is anything with truly global reach: Shakira, Metallica, 50 Cent. Whether you go with that or the standard meaning outlined above, version 2.0 presents alternatives to both—emissions from the flip side where vocals recorded in slapdash studios get released online and aired on sound systems that same night. By the next day, the track has been sampled again by a crew on the other side of the world and mashed up with whatever concoctions they've got going on. In a so-called attention economy, what better way to prove that you've paid attention to something than to remix it? Meet the folk music of the twenty-first century.

Authorial ambition doesn't drive this music, mutation does. Writing "original" songs isn't a goal or concern. Most producers begin remixing existing material, and for many, that's as far as they get. Some do even less: they simply rename MP3s in attempts to pass off the product as their own. Impersonators, plagiarists, and outright thieves are far harder to catch when everyone's work spreads via pseudonyms and sketchy file-sharing services, and when most participants never expect to meet the others face-to-face.

Any mix-and-match Frankenstein you can think of has probably been created, from Uzbekistani R&B to West African hiplife. Accordions and African techno? It's called *funaná*, and German DJ crews have started uploading their version of it too. Rap in indigenous languages is classic World Music 2.0, and there's more of it every day, beaming out from villages such as Issafen, Morocco. Electricity arrived there in 2003; today Tamazigh-language MCs record their freestyles on cell phones.

Songs circulate online among fans for whom an MP3 player set to Shuffle trumps conventional genre as an organizing principle. Refined tastes intertwine with semi-random surf trails to become indistinguishable from each other. Timelines fray, genealogies wander. These under-the-radar exchanges generally happen outside commercial spheres, adding to the fertile mess. You must sift through a lot of junky MP3s to uncover the great ones, but in the end, all the world's sonic secrets are out there, clumped irregularly across the Internet's flat and mighty sprawl. A catchy genre name or evocative creation myth can make the output of a few friends appear as a bustling scene to outside eyes, and the online hype can turn into a self-fulfilling prophecy if global excitement trickles down into actual gigs.

Restless DJs gravitated to World Music 2.0 first, driven by one-upmanship, curiosity, and a predilection for thinking of songs as building blocks. Who else has time to spend hours plumbing the Net's bottomless oceans in search of the occasional pearl? Scant opportunities exist for fans to purchase this music.

Like any city, the Internet has its outskirts: you live there if you don't understand English, if you only get online on other people's devices, if your connection is sluggish. Much music fueling World Music 2.0 comes from these outskirts. As participants in a fully networked musical system—don't call it a genre—loud, Net-savvy listeners exert more influence and earn more money from World Music 2.0 than do its producers, who live on the edges of the network. The fundamental asymmetry of the Web shapes World Music 2.0.

World Music 2.0 is an Internet-native structure that hews to the logic of the information economy. Knowing where to find it is more valuable than making it. The artists fade into the background, equal parts content provider and ghost. Meanwhile the protagonist is the compiler, the DJ-digger, the listener who is getting down.

The best of it, or at least the best connected, migrates from local obscurity to the velvet-rope clubs of London, Berlin, and New York. The songs, that is—rarely do the music makers themselves get to take advantage of their erratic global fame. Powerful centralizing figures can swoop down to capitalize on the messy underconnected currents of World Music 2.0, either by rebranding them outright (as M.I.A. did with Wilcannia Mob) or by aping the style without uplifting any of its originators. That an outspoken middleman can have more impact on a song's meaning and reception than the people who created it is one of World Music 2.0's defining paradoxes.

All hail the digital cornucopia! Pay no attention to the plastic aftertaste.

At its worst, World Music 2.0 offers the clubland equivalent of a package vacation. At its best, it propels some of the most exciting music in the world.

THE CAIRO BEAT

For the last several years an electrifying new style has been emerging from Egypt. With spot-on World Music 2.0 logic, it harnesses the quintessentially Egyptian *baladi* rhythm to hip-hop-style beat turnarounds, repetitive synthesizer riffs, and shimmering auto-tuned vocals midway between rapping and singing. They call this giddy, effervescent sound *mahraganat* (festival). Unlike lots of the North African electronic music I admire, which tends to make few concessions to audiences outside the region, *mahraganat* cribs ideas from R&B and rap, and shares their default 4/4 time signature, which makes it much easier to DJ in sets of other global electronic dance music. When a fan in Cairo first tipped me off about the scene, YouTube videos with rowdy comment sections were the main source of online information. My favorite *mahraganat* came from the prolific producer (and soccer fan) DJ Figo, and after confirming that he was one of the scene's prime movers, I went scrambling to Egypt to find out more.

The first thing I learned upon arrival was that Cairo's 20 million inhabitants live in a complicated symbiosis with their 2 million cars. The constant cough and rumble they make together is as unstoppable as the roar of the sea. Despite its ferocity, Cairene traffic rarely jams, in part because drivers and pedestrians alike do not heed traffic lights, choosing instead to operate in a spongy, perilous state of advanced interpenetration where Brownian motion meets grace-under-pressure. It is a minor triumph for a newcomer to cross the street in Cairo and not have it feel like a minor triumph. I'd stand curbside, waiting for my break, and watch in horror as young children blithely stepped into oncoming traffic. Cars slowed, or swerved, and despite everyone's apparent nonchalance, in some miracle of physics or society the kids got to the other side. (Later I'd read the World Health Organization's report on how Egyptian traffic claims about twelve thousand lives a year.) And the drivers were constantly honking. These weren't sporadic bleats of irritation like one hears in the streets of America; it was a more fundamental sound: *Coming through, be aware!* Horn as sonic signal buoy. I beep therefore I am. The cumulative effect raises the city's noise-floor, ramping up the ambient stress and forcing all other sound sources—sidewalk vendors, radios, mosque loudspeakers—to ratchet themselves up several decibels to be heard.

Cars are *loud*. In this sense the Futurists, Italy's most stylish fascists, got what they wanted: chaotic machine noise blanketing the city, jackhammers in the opera. Imagine if cars were as quiet as bikes? More pedestrians would get hit by vehicles they didn't hear approaching, true, but I bet that the citywide lowering of blood pressure levels would more than make up for it, and then we'd be able to hear whatever rich sound life lies buried under car culture's omnipresent whines, squeals, whooshes, revs, screeches, and beeps.

Miraculously, a life-form evolved out of this automotive

noise ocean. The self-regulating traffic mayhem took on a mind of its own over the last few decades; the distributed intelligence of Cairo's traffic grid slowly grasped patterns in the noise and then fostered consensus on what particular combinations of long and short beeps meant. Dusty, overcrowded, and hot, beset by sporadic barricades and construction, the network of Cairo's streets spontaneously generated a language for itself. Functioning like a crude Morse code, car-horn patterns began to convey specific messages. The small vocabulary that emerged paid special attention to vulgarities. Rhythm is the grammar of this human-car speech. In fact, a program such as FruityLoops is a great way to transcribe this language.

Depending on traffic, the birthplace of *mahraganat* is located anywhere from thirty minutes to an hour and a half outside the capital, in a rough-and-tumble urban satellite called Al Salam City. There I caught up with Ahmed Farid, aka DJ Figo, as he sipped anise tea with his crew at an open-air café. Figo and friends were fresh faced and confident, dressed in bright combinations that merged American hip-hop style with Cairo street swagger. The café's other patrons looked drab in comparison, old men killing time smoking cigarettes and the occasional *shisha* water pipe, their faces turned toward a horizon blocked by endless apartment rows. It was 1:00 a.m. in the cement-and-sand outskirt city. The waiting room of a nearby twenty-four-hour X-ray clinic was packed; someone was getting a trim at the hair salon next door; and the vintage sound of Umm Kulthum's perfect voice poured out from a café speaker. Even three decades after her death, the diva remains omnipresent, but after a day of listening to the synthy, auto-tuned beats pioneered by DJ Figo, she started to sound downright ancient.

"Before Figo, there was no music," said Smiley, a round-faced LMFAO fan wearing a tweed cap. Smiley was just one in an extended crew who'd congregated around Figo as he strolled through his hometown. He wasn't the only guy in Al Salam City to have called Figo a something-from-nothing inventor in my time there. At twenty, Figo bypassed his predecessors and their reliance on traditional musicality and showed Egypt what it can sound like to make music with nothing but a computer.

History looms crushingly large in Egypt, where the present can often seem like a footnote to a majestic past. The same goes for its music: classical Egyptian greats such as Kulthum dominated the international Arabic market for most of the twentieth century, but Figo found a way to make his songs feel like more than a musical aside, influenced by predecessors such as Ahmed Adaweya, a musician who gained widespread fame in the 1970s for popularizing a sweaty, roughneck sound called sha3by (literally, "of the people"), sung in an workaday dialect as opposed to elegant high Arabic.

Ten years ago Egyptian sha3by would have been spelled shaabi or chaabi. Writing Arabic on English-charactered cell phones and computer keyboards gave rise to an ingenious vernacular form. It goes by several names, including Arabizi and Arabish. Local-dialect Arabic varies so drastically from region to region that speakers from different countries often can't understand each other. Adding to that confusion, dialect Arabic is traditionally unwritten. There's no standard way to write it down. Enter Arabizi.

Arabizi combines the Latin alphabet with numerals to phonetically spell out colloquial Arabic. The setup effectively allows its speakers to express themselves across texts and chatspeak in everyday Arabic, with more accurate pronunciations to boot. Some fear that Arabizi threatens Arabic-script literacy. Others praise it as a ground-up techno-social innovation bringing Arabic into the twenty-first century. Both sides are right: the clever hybrid makes for something simultaneously more localized and more global. I think of festival as a musical equivalent to Arabizi.

In 2006, Figo began searching "how to make beats" on YouTube. He doesn't speak English, so studying screenshots had to suffice. His creations maintained the antisentimental and ultralocal attitude of *sha3by* while electrifying it with imported genres such as hip-hop and techno. "We learn what the songs are about by watching the videos," explained rapper Alaa Fifty Cent.

Figo and Alaa Fifty made their public debut at a city festival in 2007, and by sundown the following day, their inadvertent hit single, "Al Salam City Festival," was rippling beyond Cairo. It's easy to understand why: the rugged *baladi* rhythms, ever popular at weddings, shed their folksy connotations when programmed on drum machines. Crunk-compatible synth lines played in Eastern scales brighten this new sonic landscape, while sub-bass provides oomph and Auto-Tune covers up any pitchiness in the vocals.

Stores don't carry it, the radio won't play it, but festival has become the heartbeat of Cairo's urban sprawl. It blasts out of minibuses and tuk-tuk taxis across the African megacity. It can be heard wafting out from the low-rent pleasure boats cruising the Nile and transmits itself via the most mobile sound systems of all: cell phones.

Amr Mohamed was working as a PC repairman and selling personalized ringtones on the side in the nearby city of Ain Shams when he first heard Figo's "Al Salam City Festival." Suddenly, a world of sonic possibility opened up to him. His facility with software made it easy to splice genres and coax Western synthesizers into the intricate quarter-tone tuning of Eastern *maqam* scales. Mohamed dubbed himself Amr 7a7a (in Arabizi the number 7 denotes the breathy sound of Arabic's aspirated *h*), and within a year, his productions propelled him to the top of the festival scene, a new rival to DJ Figo. A brief but intense beef flared, with the artists quickly realizing that joining forces made more sense. Mohamed, the taciturn IT guy, was complemented perfectly by Figo's gregarious magnetism, not to mention his stable of hungry MCs. Now they work and perform together, with 7a7a making a daily two-hour commute to Figo's studio in Al Salam City.

Viewed from above, Al Salam resembles a modernist grid. After the 1992 earthquake left fifty thousand homeless, the Egyptian army hastily erected brutalist apartment blocks in the middle of a desert plain. More than twenty years later, the buildings have petrified into permanence, while their inhabitants sculpt the city, quietly affirming that the real revolution is not in Tahrir Square, but any place where bleak government structures humanize and bloom with ground-up creativity. An alleyway becomes a wedding hall, a rooftop doubles as a pigeon coop, the space around a PlayStation under an awning expands to become a communal living room. In Figo's case, a storage unit on the corner of the building where he and his family live became the recording studio where he invented his music. The entry is marked FIGO in crude green brushstrokes. There's no door, only a metal grate that they keep half-raised when the studio is in session.

Inside it was cramped with stacked speakers and illuminated by single blacklight. Figo powered up his laptop, confirming the worst: his dubious Windows installation had collapsed into a data swirl of Arabic, Russian, and English gibberish. Even harder to root out than self-replicating malware are the Facebook grifters who impersonate DJ Figo and 7a7a online. At last count, there were seven fake Figo Facebook pages, a natural by-product of festival's surging popularity, especially in a country long accustomed to rumor and misinformation. Amr 7a7a's laptop ran without issue, and he fiddled with a mixer and equalizer, ignoring the friends who came in off the street to say hello.

Gradually, the hangout focused. 7a7a sent a sleek riddim looping out of the speakers on repeat, grinning like a mad scientist in the pallid glow of his computer screen. A rising festival duo from a few towns over had insulted Figo's mother via

YouTube. Alaa, fellow rapper Sadat, and Figo were biting back with a catchy retort song. They swapped verses, their vocals slick with Auto-Tune. This type of aesthetic combat keeps festival strong. Together they transformed the blacklit storage unit into a laboratory, or maybe an incubator.

Not everybody sees it this way. "They just bang on a computer until it sounds good!" said translator Ahmed Shawka. Like many Egyptians, Shawka hears this latest development in *sha3by* as nothing but unskilled noise. But it's precisely because you can make *mahraganat* without formal musical training that the Al Salam City kids are able to produce a sound describing what it is to be young in Egypt's wired and uncertain times. Festival was never intended to be political music, but the Egyptian revolution inadvertently changed the way it was viewed. In fact, you can find *sha3by* inside the Arab Spring's most famous slogan: *"Al-sha'b yurid isqaat al-nizam!"* (The people want to bring down the regime!) "The people" stems from the same root, and with it come revolutionary notions about giving the working class more of a say in how the Arab world's most populous country is run. Figo's crew flipped this slogan brilliantly, turning it into an infectious posse cut called "Al-sha'b Yurid Khamsa Genei Raseed" (The People Want Five Pounds Phone Credit). Sadat and their friend Ahmed Habib wrote the lyrics in Egyptian street Arabic, which is as different from the modern standard Arabic of the original slogan as a rap verse is from a television newscast. "The people want something new," sing Figo, Sadat, Alaa Fifty, and Hussein Ghandy. "The people want five

pounds phone credit / The people want to bring down the regime / But the people are so damn tired."

Throughout 2011, activists, onlookers, and international media
transformed the traffic circle known as Tahrir Square into an
agora, the focal point for the revolution that ousted President
Mubarak. A full spectrum of protest musicians used Tahrir as
a stage, from Pete Seeger–styled oud strummers to Islamists or
rappers folding social criticism into staccato Arabic rhymes in
"get out and vote" anthems. Festival is sly and impatient with
the political sloganeering that sounds out in Tahrir Square, and
there's also a generational divide: Mubarak was president for
twenty-nine years, longer than many festival fans have been alive.
More concerned with a savvy, scrappy worldview than with doling
out prescriptions for how to live, festival is in tune with the
city's shakily democratic subconscious. Figo and his friends
voice what a city of underdogs feels, and as the ecstatic digital
arm of the people's music, festival makes more sense than ever in
a postrevolutionary Cairo whose Arab Spring activism has
cooled into the authoritarian crackdowns of Arab Winter.

When I was there, one obvious result of Al Salam City's
sound's taking hold was the start of a weekly festival party in
downtown Cairo. Every Saturday, crowds gathered at the After
Eight bar a few blocks from Tahrir. Drink minimums priced
out the average fan, so the room filled with moneyed Cairenes
and curious expats. In the absence of a stage, MCs hopped up
on a dark windowsill to hype the cheering crowd. This sort of

event, a *sha3by* party in a swank downtown bar, would have been unthinkable a few years ago. The social stigma held that only shantytown roughs would want to hear this music. The party has since shut down, but in an underlying cultural shift, the people's music is starting to move crowds all over the country.

Still, festival remains most exciting at its birthplace. And never more so than at a street wedding. A rambunctious Tuesday-night reception for Figo's brother featured various lit-up disco floors, a separate bride-and-groom zone for photos, and a giant sound system with bone-rattling subwoofers. Figo and his crew crowded one of three stages erected in what was essentially a dirt alley between adjacent apartment buildings. A large flatscreen TV above their heads displayed Dutch superstar DJ Tiësto in concert. The mic controllers praised the family and freestyled about friendship and love. A drummer tried to keep up with the frantic electronic beats, occasionally in lockstep, occasionally in chaotic counterpoint. The all-male dance floor heaved as smaller groups broke out into coordinated steps. Fireworks scented the air with gunpowder, which mingled with the tang of hash and tobacco. Gyroscopic lights and dancing green lasers illuminated this pop-up desert discotheque, while a remote-controlled boom-arm camera swooped and dove above the crowd, recording everything for the DVD. A proud father handed out bottles of Sprite (this was a dry celebration). Women gathered in the surrounding balconies.

"Al Salam City is a beautiful place," affirmed Smiley, who was still trailing with the posse as we left the celebration. After a ten-minute walk along the dirt avenues toward a corner where the pavement begins and taxis linger, two guys in a pickup made an unusually aggressive driving maneuver. Smiley turned and said, "They're not Al Salam. Ignore them." The taxi that ushered us back to Cairo was playing DJ Figo.

5

RED BULL GIVES YOU WINGS

In 2008, a compilation CD of songs by iconic downtown NYC art rockers Sonic Youth went on sale—exclusively at Starbucks. Lead guitarist Thurston Moore peppered his speech with awkward disclaimers as fans cried foul: "I guess, for some, Sonic Youth represents something that they don't really equate with Starbucks . . . Sonic Youth has always, in a way, made itself available to the super-mainstream. In a way, Sonic Youth has a branded name." Once known for intelligently brutal songs that evoked the dark underbelly of the American Dream, Sonic Youth has now adopted both the language and format of corporate United States. Thurston Moore had approached Starbucks, not the other way around. For some fans, those developments were a lot more disturbing than the group's weird guitar tunings ever were.

When *The Boston Globe* asked him to respond to people saying that he'd sold out, Moore spat back, "There's no difference between working with Starbucks and working with record labels like Universal and Geffen. It's a knee-jerk reaction from PC watchdogs. I mean, really, which long-distance company do you use for your cell phone? Are you on the grid? If you're off the grid, I'll listen to you." I can almost hear him continuing, "If you're on the grid, I hope you're on Sprint mobile, now offering over fifty percent off on competitors' rates for those looking to switch . . ." Moore's hissy fit marked how far we'd traveled from the proud DIY spirit of the 1990s to the corporate-cuddling relativism of the 2000s.

My first encounter with branding money occurred in 2003 at a springtime festival in Pontevedra, Spain. I walked onstage and came face-to-face with an enormous glowing Red Bull logo built directly into the DJ booth. Under ordinary circumstances a DJ booth is an actual booth that overlooks the dance floor, crammed with the necessary gear. This grim monstrosity was a constructivist podium-table made from gunmetal aluminum held together at sharp angles. Centered under the decks and mixer was the glowing Red Bull logo, which couldn't be switched off. Ugh. Nobody had told me about this. I wasn't in the mood to be sponsored by Red Bull on that night or any other, so I carefully draped my jacket over the sign and started my set. Minutes later

a festival official materialized onstage, flanked by a security
guard. Gesturing and shouting with a sour-milk face, he made
it obvious to me and everyone watching that I was to spin records over an uncovered Red Bull logo or not at all. Explaining
(curtly) that I hadn't been notified about the ad, I held my
ground. Eventually I won: the jacket stayed, the goons shuffled
off, the crowd cheered, and the festival didn't pull the plug on
me as threatened.

A related but slightly less victorious scene took place in
Lima, Peru, a few years later. I was there to give a free show at
one of the city's largest cultural centers, the Fundación Telefónica, owned and heavily subsidized by the Spanish telecom
giant. A nasty labor strike greeted me when I showed up to check
out the space a day prior to my performance: hundreds of Telefónica workers blockaded the entrance to the building, staring
down a busload of riot cops armed with semiautomatic weapons. As we got whisked through an inconspicuous side entrance,
a friend hastily explained that Telefónica had recently targeted a
group of union workers with abrupt, unexplained layoffs and a
level of workplace harassment that would have been roundly
illegal just about anywhere else in the western hemisphere. The
staff inside assured me that this was the final day of protest.

Even if the protest did disperse in time, I wasn't thrilled to be
playing a set on behalf of union busters. Then again, Telefónica
had flown me down and promised a decent fee. That support
effectively financed the rest of my South American tour. Musicians have long operated in a space of bracketed freedom—I

thought of the bebop jazz musicians of the 1950s and '60s, black visionaries who used formal complexity to articulate a brazen freedom of expression that was otherwise denied to them in Jim Crow America; I thought of the stage as a place where the breaking of aesthetic rules is encouraged—so long as it doesn't interfere with business as usual in the outside world; I thought of my performance fee. *¡Mierda!* I needed that cash. And let's be honest, corporate support was the only way I could give a free experimental DJ performance in Peru in front of hundreds of people, complete with cool live video projections of my hands working the decks and mixer. I sympathized with those striking workers, but as an outsider parachuting in, I couldn't have done anything. For all Telefónica's work practices, my appearance also meant that a curator and technical staff got paid for their labor that day.

I did the show. I gave the performance all I had, an intense and unconventional set the likes of which, as many people told me afterward, had never before been seen in Lima. That afternoon, instead of union protesters, a different crowd of people were outside the Fundación Telefónica: dozens who couldn't enter once the place had filled to capacity were straining to listen through the closed glass doors. I ended my set with a turntablist cut-up of a 7-inch that I was given by a fan at the Pontevedra show, popular throughout the Spanish-speaking world: Jeanette's "Yo Soy Rebelde" (I'm a Rebel), a teen anthem from 1971. The crowd burst into applause. *On the decks*, I thought, *sure, I'm a rebel*.

It goes deeper. A decade after my first encounter with the energy drink's promotional arm, I'm skyping with three members of the Red Bull Music Academy's Berlin team. Trying not to appear eager as I hit 'em up for money. This requires some explaining.

I had been attempting to raise funds for my music software–as–art project, *Sufi Plug Ins*. The closest I'd come was a grant that Rhizome at the New Museum told me they'd give me, even announcing it discreetly on their website, provided that I restructure the project to make it more attractive to their sponsor, Deutsche Bank. As I weighed the pros and cons of the condition-heavy offer (pro: some money; con: I'd need to relocate it to NYC instead of Cairo and work with "an underserviced community" there—banks love euphemisms and the poor), their e-mails to me dwindled out, becoming less committal, then less frequent, finally fading into silence. Arts-grant applications are the saddest dances an artist knows.

Every time I mentioned the difficulty of developing *Sufi Plug Ins*, someone would tell me: Hit up Red Bull. (What global beverage brand wouldn't want to align itself with Sufi-themed electronic music software featuring an incomprehensible interface and no instructions?) The specter of that glowing lump of techno-fascist DJ furniture from Pontevedra tugged at my mind as I reflected on how much had changed.

Red Bull Music Academy (RBMA) is the energy drink's music marketing arm. They sponsor music "academies" across the globe—two weeks or so of all-expenses-paid music intensives if you are accepted, but the epic application doubles as an in-depth marketing survey that collects detailed information about the clothing, music, and entertainment choices of legions of ambitious young producers. In addition to the namesake workshops, RBMA is increasingly known for staging festivals around the world. Their curatorial approach balances buzz-worthy new acts with older groups whose presence deepens a sense of historical legacy. What felt like ham-fisted opportun-ism in Pontevedra had matured into something disarmingly respectful of dance music's fleeting trends and underdocu-mented pasts. All in all, RBMA event production has proven itself to be a classy operation, one from which similarly sized festivals in the States could learn a lot, as they tend to be far less adventuresome.

In 2013, RBMA debuted what would become a yearly monthlong festival in New York City. Word on the street put the budget at $50 million. It was serious. They even hired jour-nalists to write contextual essays related to the performances and printed them up as a free daily newspaper. America doesn't have significant government arts subsidies like in Europe, so the brief taste left many, many music industry folks in NYC tantalized by the power of Red Bull patronage. Which might have explained why everyone kept telling me to go to them.

Fact is, if Red Bull had decided to back my project, *they would have backed my project*, not asked me to switch continents and redirect my focus as the museum money had. Arts grants often ask you to bend your proposal into something that is institu-tionally pleasing; corporate money generally wants you to keep being you. Red Bull Music Academy backing appeared down-right ethical compared to the murky strings-attached grant from Deutsche Bank via Rhizome at the New Museum, whose curator had evaporated by then anyhow.

So I drafted up a zippy PDF proposal for the RBMA guys. On his lunch break from doing kitty-litter ads, my midtown Manhattan corporate-designer buddy made it look slick. The PDF piqued RBMA's interest enough to warrant a conference video call with three members of their Berlin team. Three people! I could practically smell the money. Moments after Skype con-nected, I knew I was wrong. Amid image dropouts and crispy audio, I watched myself watch the three men watch me. Video-chat technology is good at making bad meetings worse. Zero energy was in the air. They were nice enough; I suspect that it didn't go over as bad as it felt, but after five minutes I couldn't figure out why they'd opted to speak with me in the first place. By the end of the conversation it was clear there would be no follow-ups. I'd rejected Red Bull in Pontevedra; now Red Bull was rejecting me. ¯_(ツ)_/¯

Don't smile, it's postmodern.

As a long-term corporate project supporting inspired music, the Red Bull Music Academy remains unparalleled. Yet all manner of brands have refined their techniques for cozying up to artists since the early 2000s. Before then, no large companies backed unknown artists. Now these artists are seen as vital in-fluencers, well worth brands' spending up to a third of their ad-vertising budget on music sponsorships. However, this is only part of the deal. Musicians also provide a context in which

one's product can be displayed, however casually. Celebrity en-
dorsement deals are expensive, and extremely rare. Beyoncé's
2012 deal with Pepsi paid out $50 million. Against numbers like
that, budgeting a few thousand to throw shows at Austin's
SXSW festival, or to cover videographer costs for a musician's
promo reel, is chump change. Perhaps literally: if you believe
that brand sponsorship is selling out, then more people are doing
it now than ever before, for less than ever. It's telling that these
companies go out of their way to assure us that they don't own
any of the music produced. They appear generous as they let us
know that our music is literally worthless to them. It's embed-
dedness in our little cultures that they want. Our musical ac-
tivities provide a context in which the brands can be seen. We
provide the site, arenas of relevance that stretch from social media exchanges to video clips to club nights and tours. Our
sounds and struggles activate their environs as places of heightened meaning; all the brands need to do is hang out unobtru-
sively in that charged space.

Red Bull has convinced people they're a culture company
that also sells energy drinks as opposed to the reverse, which is
a stunning success. The more hands-off and discreet their presence is, the more they appear as cultural agents in support of a
scene. They're cool too! Our music's perceived lack of value becomes a self-fulfilling prophecy: one of the reasons that artists
are expected to seek brand "partnerships" is because it's so difficult for musicians to earn a living selling music or touring
nowadays. The corporate largesse is both symptom and proof
of this worthlessness.

I put *partnerships* in quotes because how the corporate world redefines it has much to do with what's going on here. Musical groups can provide a great example of interdependent partnerships: individuals pooling their unique talents to create something that's greater than the sum of its parts. Fandom relies on this identification, even when it doesn't reflect the way a particular group is run. Brand-artist partnerships are an altogether different arrangement: a large business entity enlisting the support of a few artists, more concerned with market penetration than teamwork. Businesses can partner with each other because the playing field is relatively level. But corporations partnering with musicians? It's absurd. By using the word to apply to corporations' dealings with musicians, these distinct meanings of partnership blur: the companies win out, of course; they get humanized. Like the eternal refrain of someone trying to gain access to a club, "they're with the band."

Examples of this plague my in-box. It's not the brands that spam me, it's the musicians or their publicists. Here's one from today, where the rappers' newsletter spliced in chunks of third-party marketing copy: "'Our partnership with Run The Jewels represents our belief in supporting those that don't care about the status quo and stay focused on their own vision,' says Volcom Global Creative Director . . . Check out Run the Jewels talking about the culture that unites them with Volcom here and be on the lookout for more RTJ x Volcom coming very soon!"

Run the Jewels is the highly regarded indie rap duo of NYC's rapper/producer El-P and Atlanta's Killer Mike; Volcom seems to make jeans. Whatever Volcom is, a YouTube video of Run the Jewels having a blast on tour showcases "the culture that unites them." At every step these partnerships urge us to disregard music's worth. You're there to buy energy drinks or jeans, not some song. The Volcom/RTJ video is called "Run the Jewels: In Pursuit of a Real Life Happening." The last thing the company wants to do is lock down its brand to an album! Experience is all.

In 1958 artist and writer Allan Kaprow coined the term *happening* to refer to a new kind of art event where the barrier separating viewer from creator melted away and the ephemeral held more importance than any material object. "The blurring of art and life," he enthused. Kaprow was right, albeit in ways he couldn't have imagined.

The Converse sneaker company opened an enormous music recording studio where select unsigned bands can record for free. Sour Patch Kids underwrites a crash-pad apartment for musicians. London retailer Rough Trade opened up a store and performance space where entry is sometimes free with an album purchase. Those examples are just in Brooklyn. Over in Manhattan, RBMA unveiled a studio to rival the sneaker company's.

Green Label Sound began as PepsiCo's attempt to connect music fans with their fluorescent Mountain Dew drink. Their language is typical: "Green Label Sound is a record label curated by Mountain Dew, designed to elevate and empower independent artists." Toyota started a record label–cum–lifestyle marketing division called Scion AV, a prominent sponsor of DJ tours in the United States. One season I noticed Fiat is trying to catch up, partly by poaching Scion-sponsored DJs to play Fiat promo parties. If the government ever legalizes weed, then artist sponsorship deals are gonna get extra-crazy.

The spiritual father of these developments is Richard "Moby" Hall. In 1999, the electronica producer released an album that he'd recorded in his Manhattan apartment. *Play* received little attention until the licensing began. Advertisements, film sound tracks, theme songs, TV interlude music: within a year of its release, *Play* was sold off for all these uses and more. Moby made history as the first artist to license every single song from an album. That unprecedented exposure fueled more than 12 million album sales. A dizzying array of global brands helped transform the white techno DJ into America's first mainstream electronic music star.

Play's liner notes contain short essays by Moby on veganism (good), fundamentalism (bad), and his version of Christianity (it's complicated)—but not consumerism. Licensing the music so widely never presented him with an ethical dilemma. I found *Play* upsetting not because its core sonic identity comes from the voices of old African American blues singers that Moby sampled and layered with atmospheric beats, but rather because brands such as American Express, Rolling Rock, Baileys Irish Cream, Nissan, Volkswagen, Renault, and many more were so ready to use those cushy decontextualizations to advertise their products.

Moby didn't sell out, but he did insert his wares into a system that trades on the appearance of authenticity. Of course, black soulfulness repackaged and sold by whites is the very antithesis of what we understand as authenticity—but, as with *Play*, that mediation consistently makes it more rather than less sellable. The catchiest moments of *Play* are built on the voices of poor southern blacks, recorded decades earlier by Alan Lomax. The blues voices that loop inside Moby's pop-friendly arrangements remind us that the central fact of black authenticity in America is dispossession. Which makes *Play* a profoundly American album, and Moby, with his heart-on-sleeve diatribes and full complicity with this complex machinery, a transitional figure.

REAL ROCK STARS DO THEIR OWN LAUNDRY

Moby's licensing coup marks a huge shift from the nineties, when selling out seemed possible because "doing it yourself" with integrity was a reality. *Play*-era Moby was fond of wearing a Minor Threat T-shirt for TV interviews, in homage to the American hardcore band and its principled leader, Ian MacKaye. The brands aligned themselves with Moby; Moby aligned himself with MacKaye, an artist whose path, particularly in his second group, Fugazi, gave us one of the most poignant and influential visions of what a DIY approach might accomplish.

The roots of Fugazi reach back to Washington, D.C., in 1980, the year seventeen-year-old MacKaye founded Minor Threat. This was a grim time in rock music history: the painfully awkward years between the glory of the late-sixties-era Stones and Beatles and the 1992 emergence of Nirvana—in a nutshell, the era when glossy hair metal bands were selling out football stadiums. Even punk rock was still in its infancy: barely five years had passed since the Sex Pistols had declared anarchy in the U.K. The species of punk that migrated to the United States between 1975 and 1980 was heavily indebted to the iconography established by the Sex Pistols: sneering, leather-clad nihilists with Mohawks and safety-pin piercings, starting fights onstage, throwing up onstage, barely making it through their sets.

This nascent punk scene rubbed young Ian MacKaye the wrong way; he was drawn to the raw energy and aggression of punk but not to the sloppiness, the peacocking. So from the very start Minor Threat was an exercise in purification and clarity—not only in their appearance and ethos (logo-less T-shirts; shaved heads; absolutely no drugs, alcohol, or fluorescent energy drinks), but also in their stripped-down, intensified sound. MacKaye sang-shouted anthemic lyrics—perfect for sing-alongs with his high school friends, the initial core audience members—as he cranked out chunky riffs on guitar. American hardcore was born. And while Minor Threat began by playing high school cafeterias and local VFW halls, within a year their reputation spread and they began touring widely, leaving a wake of ringing ears and near-mythic stories about the free-for-all energy of their live shows. Crucially, though, they never abandoned their foundational principles: devotion to the local scene, personal integrity, and affordable all-ages shows (the band members themselves were too young to be admitted to 21+ clubs). From the outset Mac-Kaye was a messianic figure, a charismatic, curmudgeonly mentor around whom a nationwide scene was built, comprising young punks, skaters, and music geeks connected via photocopied zines, independent record shops, and word-of-mouth touring networks.

Rising success didn't make things easier. Artistic tensions ran high, exacerbated by what the band members saw as the declining quality of the hardcore scene. Their vision for rowdy, community-strengthening catharsis had devolved into concerts soured by meatheads looking to pick fights. By 1983, less than three years after they began, Minor Threat had broken up.

Four years later, Ian MacKaye reemerged from a period of relative silence and formed Fugazi. Whereas Minor Threat belted out overt political and moral declarations with infectious adolescent confidence, Fugazi questioned, probed, opened up possibilities. They moved seamlessly between moments of fierce punk intensity, experimental soundscapes, and angular funk. Guy Picciotto and MacKaye traded open-ended, abstract lyrics as they sparred on guitars. Bassist Joe Lally injected a sense of spaciousness borrowed from dub reggae. Brendan Canty's drumming was equally indebted to hardcore's 4/4 metronomic sprint as to the swinging funk of black D.C.'s go-go bands.

Early Fugazi sounded like nobody else, and they knew it; they also knew that they had to tour constantly and win their audience over one by one, fan by fan. The gig lists from 1988 and '89 suggest that they played a show somewhere in America just about every night. Their democratic approach to songwriting, combined with a formidable tour schedule, honed Fugazi into a transfixing live band. They matured hardcore's intensity beyond youthful aggression, a shift that enabled them to reach a wider audience and sell more units than most major-label acts. Their success was aided by the transference of MacKaye's strident antiestablishment views onto professional ethics: $5 all-ages shows at humble venues, no violent moshing, no T-shirts or merchandise for sale, no unnecessary expenses, no advertising except in local zines, no interviews with media sources they themselves didn't read. By 1994 they became figureheads for the rising indie scene; a young Kurt Cobain and Michael Stipe were vocal supporters.

Fugazi has sold roughly 2 million records to date with little to no advertising, all on their own Dischord label, and have done multiple global headlining tours, regularly selling out cavernous venues. Although they went on indefinite hiatus in 2003, to this day they refuse lucrative offers to use their material in advertisements or Hollywood films, or to headline festivals such as Coachella, which paid the Pixies a cool million for their reunion set in 2004.

Gifted musicianship made this all possible, but so too did their reliance on (and belief in) DIY strategies, what I like to call hand-to-hand combat: direct actions done with a sense of responsibility to the greater musical community. It comes in many forms. Hitting the road to perform at venues that were independent by necessity—a punk house, a tiny club, a Unitarian church basement, whatever worked. Selling rap mixtapes out of the trunk of a car. Schlepping to the post office twice a week to ship out mail orders, hoofing it around town to drop off merch at shops that accepted consignment. Donating time and expertise to help a friend record their album.

My favorite Fugazi story is about laundry.

The rule was, after each concert, everyone had to wash his sweaty clothes in a sink at the venue before moving on. Problem: wet clothes mildew, but Laundromats are inconvenient when you're on the road. Solution: throw a dryer in the van and take that on tour. Fugazi toured with a dryer in their van? Yes. It is so practical that it seems borderline insane. And that to me is the lasting lesson in Fugazi's extraordinary career: ethics aren't some big thing you invoke in interviews; they're how you slog through the daily grind. The devil is in the details, but mindful living is too. Fugazi's way of being in the world made sense, intuitively. Start with what you know and grow it. MacKaye is often profiled as a stern moralizer, but in my experience he's a considerate guy who believes in pitching in so that those around him do what they do better.

I met MacKaye in D.C. when his friends' band and I were on the same bill. A couple of guys were onstage during my soundcheck setup, and out of the blue MacKaye offered to help me move gear around. I'd recently returned from doing a live sound track with Guy Picciotto in Chile, but Ian didn't know any of that at the time. I was just a guy who needed a hand, and he stepped in without my having to ask. Imagine if all rock royalty acted that way?

A code of ethics means nothing unless you're willing to lug around hard-core appliances. No worries if it's too heavy to lift: that's what community is for.

Of course, few bands had the chance to "buy in" in the sense of receiving megabucks to do something that went against their values, so selling out was never quite as easy a thing to do as it may have seemed. People understood Fugazi's career path in simpler, more applicable terms: you strengthen the networks you participate in.

Which isn't to say that things were easier back then. What has happened is that all the industry upheavals have made the ability to control the circulation of one's work a whole lot trickier. The brick-and-mortar and mail-order store infrastructure has mostly collapsed, leaving in its wake untold artists who must navigate impersonal online upload forms to sell their songs digitally. Facing a reduced buying public, the gatekeepers who still work at brick-and-mortar shops tend to stock their bins with more conservative choices than ever, in part because record labels investing in physical product can't afford to take risks either. Independent-minded musicians are expected to invest more time hyping their creations on social media than was spent making them.

As I slurp my sixteen-ounce Mountain Dew Baja Blast at the combination Pizza Hut and Taco Bell, listening through Beats earbuds to an unskippable Toyota ad serviced by Vevo that runs before Sonic Youth's "Disintegrate" video on YouTube, a subsidiary of Google, itself the lead subsidiary of holding company Alphabet Inc., I reflect on the situation. It's time to act! So I whip out my Apple iPhone with service provided by T-Mobile, a holding company for Germany's Deutsche Telekom AG, and tweet, *From Do-It-Yourself to Embed-It-Yourself . . . how did we get here?*

The short answer is, blame tabloid king Rupert Murdoch. Well, him and almost every single musician you listen to. Remember MySpace? It went online the year Fugazi broke up. These days it's just another digital ghost town. A decade ago, it was incredible. Murdoch bought it in 2005 and presided over the site through its glory years, when it was the world's biggest social network.

More than any other site in the aughts, MySpace helped independent musicians steer their self-presentation and ramp up their networking, for free. You could create your own page with a customized URL, host streaming songs, list tour dates, send private messages, maintain a blog, display your selection of "Top Friends," and more. Enlivening your page with graphics was easy. This was before Facebook, before YouTube. Musicians flocked to it en masse.

Like everybody else, I uploaded my art into Murdoch's corporate matrix. Eagerly. Profitably. I landed remix offers. I booked gigs. When I visited Buenos Aires in 2008, a handful of different artists told me how MySpace "Top Friends" surfing led them to discover kindred spirits in their city, knowledge that then seeded a new wave of club nights and music labels. Stories like this were common. In all his global ambition, Rupert Murdoch proved to be extremely good at getting things everywhere—from antennas in shantytowns aimed at Sky satellites to the construction of a platform that assisted a previously underconnected web of independent musicians around the globe. The site was so useful that we didn't think twice about how everyone's page came slathered in crappy ads. Amid our peer-to-peer chatter, those ads faded into the background noise (precisely where they do their best work).

The promise of a democratic all-access Web felt like a reality on MySpace. This was the forum of global conversation we'd all been looking for. It was fun while it lasted.

Anarchist marching bands listing their tour dates under wide-screen banners for the latest Tom Cruise franchise blockbuster should have been a clue that MySpace was not a DIY utopia. I remember seeing my latest album artwork slapped atop *Spider-Man* wallpaper. The damage was done. Hell, we'd *signed up* for it.

The ads themselves weren't a problem. If anything, they were a warning sticker. MySpace conditioned us to accept that what was previously known as underground culture was, from here on out, something that you'd discover or create by accessing a for-profit website, driven by business motives often at odds with the very cultures of sharing and communication they sought to cultivate among their user base.

The lessons of Fugazi and the cautionary tale of MySpace are more relevant than ever in our hyperconnected world. After all, do-it-yourself reflected a growing awareness of the power of participating in the creation and maintenance of a network. Websites, apps, and the like—these are all simply points in a network ultimately held together by people. Ideas are the original viral content, and voicing ideas about how we wish to relate to each other and our creations is a key step toward making change happen.

The hope is that music lovers will resuscitate the meaning of terms like *do-it-yourself* and *indie* to describe music whose distribution lies in the hands of its creators. Indie fans become those who support knowing that their money (or their "likes") will reach the artists with a minimum of third-party interference, and that the music will circulate among its audiences with a maximum of artist-friendly control.

My desires here are basic: How can I access great new tunes and ensure that their creators receive the lion's share of payment for their work? Some of the most exciting music being made right now is produced by people who can't capitalize on it because their art enthralls a microaudience of fans scattered around the world. Enterprising DJs can make money and a name for themselves by being the middlemen between the source of the hot new track and its potential audience. Which they—we—gladly do. To help the least connected musicians write the rules of their game, a properly useful DIY tool should use the power of the Web while going against the network logic that favors the well-connected.

The fact that people underestimated the speed with which cell phones would spread throughout Africa tells me that there's a world of opportunity to make something useful on top of that, for example. From Cape Town to Casablanca, phone payments have skyrocketed. I'd thrill to be able to buy songs directly from the person who made them.

I haven't studied global development. Abolishing national borders seems like a step in the right direction. Until that happens, I want 320 Kbps MP3 dance-floor heaters, and I'm willing to pay.

DISTRIBUTIONAL AESTHETICS

With Fugazi, how you heard about them and experienced their music was an integral part of who they were. That's the full story behind their refusal to be featured in *Rolling Stone*. Whoever wanted to read interviews with them could seek out the alternative media sources they championed. Simple as that. Fugazi made a conscious effort to participate in the networks that they wanted to strengthen. They could tour like maniacs to well-attended shows all over the world—and not appear in glossy magazines or in TV commercials. Call it distributional aesthetics: how your material circulates to find its audience forms a vital part of your art.

The idea gained mainstream traction in 2013, when three of pop's biggest stars each released new material in unorthodox ways. They're tightly interlinked—the power couple of Beyoncé Knowles and her husband, Shawn "Jay Z" Carter, and Kanye West, who has released six albums with Jay Z's Roc-a-Fella imprint (including his duo album with Jay Z)—which makes the differences in how they got their music out that year even more striking.

Let's start with the worst, Jay Z. That July he sold a million copies of his new album to a South Korean electronics company. Four days before the commercial release of *Magna Carta Holy Grail*, Samsung made its copies available to the first million Galaxy smartphone owners who downloaded a special app for it. The Jay Z album app was free for them, but its cost was significant: the thing data-mined its users. It required access to e-mail, phone-call, and GPS-location information. Even fans who weren't concerned with privacy issues found Jay Z's app manipulative: it would only display song lyrics if you sent out a tweet or a Facebook update for each one. The Samsung deal was yet another grimly efficient business move for Jay Z, the fella who shot his brother over a stolen ring at age twelve.

The deal garnered him $5 million before the album even hit the streets. The message it sent to his die-hard supporters who didn't have the Samsung smartphone models? You people can wait.

Jay Z set a depressing precedent that U2 was quick to follow. Their 2014 album, *Songs of Innocence*, automatically downloaded into the accounts of *half a billion* iTunes customers. Five hundred million people saddled with aging rock, with no warnings or chances to opt in. Bands, brands, and smothering pseudogenerosity: Who needs fans when you've got high-level content-provision deals with multinational technology conglomerates?

Beyoncé's approach was far more interesting. Her self-titled album appeared for sale, unannounced, on iTunes in 119 countries on December 13, 2013. A video accompanied each song. Industry convention regards December as a no-go zone for new releases, since publications will have finalized their Best of the Year lists and stores are busy trying to clear out inventory. Her surprise attack bucked that convention in grand style. The shock waves *Beyoncé* sent across the Internet were immediately followed by a collective roar of adulation. Her fan base got to react to *Beyoncé* at the same time as the critics if not before, and as expected they made an extraordinary amount of noise in service of the record.

In contrast with Jay Z's techno-paternalism, Beyoncé trusted her fans' ability to listen, react, and share. You don't need an invasive app to get people to praise Queen Bey; her status as reigning classy pop queen is more than enough. The strategy was shrewd: no need for a top-shelf publicity firm; simply outsource product promotion to paying customers, who'll do it for free. "I didn't want to release my music the way I've done it," she said. "There's so much that gets between the music, the artist, and the fans." (Such as Samsung cell phones?) *Beyoncé* became iTunes' fastest-selling album. You couldn't buy an individual song either; it was full album price or nothing.

These boss business moves perfectly complemented *Beyoncé*'s female-empowerment lyrics. The package was total. The leak-free surprise release showcased Beyoncé's control. And the secret of the secret is that you only need a few people to put files on sale at the same time across 119 countries. Or to delete them. Beyoncé's work-intensive flawlessness requires a massively centralized delivery system.

But 2013's most head-exploding moment of distributional aesthetics came from Kanye West's "New Slaves" premiere. West unveiled the single via simultaneous outdoor projection at sixty-six locations around the world. The video consisted of an extended close-up shot of Kanye rapping, projected in high-contrast black and white against iconic facades, such as midtown Manhattan's Prada store and Chicago's Wrigley Field. The projector beam illuminated as much of the building on which it was projected as it did of Kanye West. No clean images were to be seen: vocalist and site became one, and every screening looked different.

Kanye West is a master of the modern rant, and "New Slaves" found him in fine form: "Used to only be niggas, now everybody playin' / Spendin' everything on Alexander Wang." It's a screed against consumerism, vis-à-vis slavery's legacy. The only thing under Kanye's voice is a grimy synth bass line. The lack of a beat gives "New Slaves" a tension that makes his delivery even more urgent.

Kanye's presentation of "New Slaves" merged with its core message. He wasn't just rapping about turning one's back on rampant corporatization, he was enacting it by staging a one-of-a-kind performance, unrepeatable and unbuyable (at least for several months). And he staged it in public space!

"New Slaves" got distributed as a singularity, not a single. Singularity: a one-of-a-kind event, any unprecedented thing suddenly and stubbornly itself. There was no audio to stream, no "official" video version to watch, no purchase links. You either experienced "New Slaves" in person or saw one of the countless grainy cell-phone videos that were uploaded in its aftermath. Each fanvid captures the sounds of each location-specific bustle too. One hears crowd chatter, jokes, and commentary. On a handful of versions enterprising youngsters rap over Kanye.

"New Slaves" videos honored the individual points of view of his audience. The song's release played with the physical/

digital divide, breaking up the sameness (of file, of experience) that comes with online debuts. The anarchic bloom of similar but distinct, and distinctly captured experiences, was central to it. Kanye West presented "New Slaves" in such a way as to ensure that there couldn't be any definitive digital documentation. Instead we experienced a proliferation of specific positions and conditions, each bristling with the traffic and bustle of where it occurred. Much is made of Ye's bigheadedness—itself a canny marketing move—but this was a brilliant way to set "New Slaves" in circulation.

Networked reality entangles individuals and big businesses, hive minds and algorithmic processes. The Web formed is not a landscape: one cannot step back to gain perspective. We're in it as much as it's in us. New slaves dream of new freedoms. Simply by existing, truly new music asks of those who care for it, How can we set a sound aloft so that it reaches those who most need to hear it?

6

CUT & PASTE

Mixtape as flirtation device was one of the great uses of late twentieth-century recording technology. That's what I knew, pouring my heart into homemade dual-cassette-deck compilations, then Xerox-collaging cover art. So much of adolescence is spent in thrall to emotions we can't articulate, much less control. What better way than mixtapes to respond? The stories you can tell by putting the right songs in the right sequence for the right person. Later I began putting together zines. The underlying approach remained the same.

Cut and paste.

It's an impulse as old as humanity. In his delightful book

In Praise of Copying, Marcus Boon argues "that copying is a fundamental part of being human, that we could not be human without copying, and that we can and should celebrate this aspect of ourselves, in full awareness of our situation. Copying is not just something human—it is a part of how the universe functions and manifests." That "universal function" powered hip-hop, jungle, and lots of other music that set my head spinning. When I bought a sampler, my friend DJ Moosaka asked, "What's the first thing you're gonna sample? Everybody has some records they've been dying to cut up." He was right. We thought about musical creation in terms of cut and paste before we had the gear to do it. We weren't the only ones. This mix-and-match trickster spirit powered many of last century's most emblematic creative strategies.

The modern meaning of cut and paste settled into place in the early 1900s. Mass-manufactured visual culture had swept in with the industrial revolution, and artists responded by hacking apart those very images—newspaper ads, flyers, and more—in hopes that their reassembled shapes could counteract the logic of homogenizing sameness. From there the provocative art-making approach leaped across media, switching names with each jump.

At the end of World War I, Berlin dadaists coined the term *photomontage* to refer to the photographs and newspaper clippings they'd scissored into startling composite images that spoke to the shell-shocked postwar reality. Soviet directors such as Sergei Eisenstein used the jump cuts of montage as the principal tool in their political films. Texts whose authorial integrity got razor-bladed into punky palimpsests were called *cut-ups*. On it went, from photocopied zines to photoshopped memes. DJ culture runs on the stuff. By 2001 it seemed as if more people spliced incongruous pop and rock songs together into bootleg mashups than released "original" music. The surprisingly cathartic yet suspiciously short "Every Scream from Every Arnold Movie" (only seven minutes of Schwarzenegger yelling?) is a prime example of supercuts, which aggregate thematic bits from TV and movies for absurd satirical effect.

All these cats love underdog logic; cut and paste ushers it in. What better way to shake an audience—and oneself—out of the complacency that comes from familiarity and into a funkier, freer space where questions can begin?

Hannah Höch's 1919 breakout photomontage, *Cut with the Dada Kitchen Knife Through the Last Weimar Beer-Belly Cultural Epoch in Germany*, set the tone early: *cut* breaks authority's framework, *paste* inserts radical new perspectives that challenge the smooth surfaces of power, and a little humor goes a long way. Her *Cut*'s jarring pictorial space is filled with angular cityscapes and transformed bodies often limbed by machine or animal parts, all shot through with a spill of typography. Several of the disfigured images suggest the war's walking wounded; in others Höch deploys scantily clad females to derail the sexist expectation that such advertising images set up. Swimsuited female forms become no-necked beardo men. Lenin smiles as if he knows a secret, or perhaps he's just happy to be wearing the heart-patterned jumpsuit that shows off his bosom and womanly hips.

Höch revels in thwarting expectations, and cut and paste is

the only artistic technique that can actively interrupt mainstream visual logic in that way. Her work also puts cut and paste forward as reproduction—a form of birth that can escape or attack traditional gendered roles. In *Cut*'s lower right-hand corner a cutout map indicates the European countries where women had the right to vote. A photograph of the artist sits on its left edge. Citizen and individual: each is a self-portrait.

Höch was part of the early twentieth-century art movement known as dada. Dada celebrated absurdist anti-art as a reaction to the European rationalism that had spawned the horrors of World War I. The powers that be had unleashed a trauma so cutting that even basic conceptions of beauty had to be destroyed. The dadaists' concerns included distrust of "chaos vs. order" narratives, and above all, a belief that art, at its most extreme, can be a liberationist force strong enough to overwrite conservative ideas about propriety, so long as it escapes the confines of the art world. This last bit is crucial to the collage-as-provocation equation. It's not enough to tap into the materials of popular consciousness and display the results in an art gallery or avant-garde magazine. You have to set them loose in the messy public sphere too. If collages don't irritate some of the audience, then you're not putting the art where it needs to be.

BRING THE NOISE!

Cut and paste's shake-'em-up spirit reached my generation in the form of Public Enemy.

The Long Island crew made waves in the eighties as much for their bombastic, sample-heavy production as for Chuck D's bold activist rhymes. An in-house production crew led by brothers Hank and Keith Shocklee architected PE's beats under the name the Bomb Squad. Their audio collages transmitted the frame-breaking experience of the black radicals to those otherwise far removed from it. Public Enemy's ability to generate politically prickly party jams from borderline atonal sound design remains hugely influential. Their induction into the Rock and Roll Hall of Fame in 2013 spoke more of the rock institution's efforts to stay cool than to any significant accolade for the group.

Public Enemy's 1988 album, *It Takes a Nation of Millions to Hold Us Back*, and follow-up single, "Fight the Power," showcased the cut-and-paste ethos in fine form. Director Spike Lee commissioned "Fight the Power" for his 1989 film, *Do the Right Thing*. The beat is a maximalist brick comprising dozens of layered samples, dense yet eerily spry. Sample collages of this complexity took ages to assemble with 1980s hardware. "Fight the Power" conveys a sense of immediacy despite the painstakingly slow compositional process.

Rapper Chuck D's stentorian voice is bracing in its urgency. Listen carefully and underneath his lyrics you'll hear snippets of James Brown break beats, bells, street sounds, historical speeches, Bob Marley, soul singers, distorted guitar riffs, British hair metal band Uriah Heep, even a bit of an earlier Public Enemy song. The breadth of the (potentially) recognizable samples acknowledges and creates a shared slide through history—and

not some trite "black" history—Public Enemy's catholic sylla-
bus proudly includes stuff such as (all-white) Uriah Heep.

"Lemme hear you say" runs a sample—*"Fight the power!"*
yell Chuck D and court jester Flavor Flav before it finishes. It's
not an affirmational call-and-response, and it sure ain't harmony. This noisy overlap says: History is a jostling crowd. Since
the past won't stop playing, PE talks with—and over—it. A
whole lotta voices struggle to sound out. The interplay of inter-
ruptions sets the tempo. Our sound track is built from scraps.

Public Enemy used info overload as a compositional element.
Their art required a polyphony of citationally rich sounds, and
cut and paste was the only way to get there. Sample-based
hip-hop was everywhere at the time, but no others managed
to connect the strategy to larger cultural concerns the way PE
did. Indeed, the sound of Public Enemy points toward a politics
more than their lyrics do.

Kid consumers in Middle America heard and responded.
When Public Enemy began, rap was little more than NYC
outer-borough bricoleurs reciting street poetry in metered rhyme
over stripped-down drum machines or chopped-up bits of soul
albums. Little by little, the urban funk spread. PE's enormous appeal helped expand rap into a significant cultural force. By the
decade's end hip-hop had exploded into a commercial jugger-
naut worth millions. Mainstream visibility brought money, and
money brought lawyers.

In 1991, Warner Bros. sued rapper Biz Markie for using a ten-
second loop from a Gilbert O'Sullivan tune without permis-

sion. They won the case. The landmark ruling sent prohibitive copyright laws descending in full force. Virtually overnight, sampling went from being an aspirational, intertextual smash-and-grab glory to a luxury good attended to by lawyers. Public Enemy's success paradoxically helped bring about the demise of their main expressive mode: cut and paste. If you wanted samples, you had to pay—a lot.

For much of the twentieth century, collage allowed one to punch up. Can't afford studio time or art lessons? Grab scissors, get started. Collage let artists of limited means leverage pop commentary into the world. Art-making as public conversation. Skyrocketing sample-clearance costs ended that in music. Individual samples grew pricey. As for artists such as Public Enemy who relied on dozens of samples? The legal fees alone were prohibitive. Their sonic world-making was effectively legislated out of existence.

The golden process began spitting out junk.

Ten years after *Nation of Millions*, Sean Combs, aka Puff Daddy, aka P. Diddy, released "I'll Be Missing You." It charted instantly and remains his most popular song to date. This is largely because it's built around the famous guitar riff from "Every Breath You Take." Who hasn't heard the Police's Grammy-winning megahit? Diddy's work traded on that instant recognition.

In terms of cut and paste, "I'll Be Missing You" is pretty much the least interesting thing one can do. The schlocky tune is so devoid of contrarian potential that Diddy didn't seem to register that the Police original is a "sinister" song about "surveillance and control," as Sting put it. Diddy says that his song pays tribute to slain Brooklyn rapper the Notorious B.I.G., yet "I'll Be Missing You" can more accurately be said to pay tribute to Sting. If anything, "I'll Be Missing You" helps us to forget Biggie: neither his voice nor his music (which Diddy owns) appear in the song.

Combs nabbed the Police sample without permission and was subsequently forced to cede the majority of its profits to Sting. This was a double coup for the British star, as the key sample contains none of his contributions to the Police song. Andy Summers composed and performed the guitar line. Due to band disputes he was never credited and thus earns nothing from the original or its sampling, whereas Sting has received tens of millions of dollars for "Every Breath You Take" and continues to make a profit of around $2,000 a day from it.

The episode illustrates how thoroughly the oppositional ethos at the heart of cut and paste got drained. Sampling teams up with copyright law to reinforce lame ideas of authority.

Nowadays when Kanye West incorporates a few seconds of Nina Simone or Otis Redding, it's no longer about brilliant theft or noisy homage—it's West flashing a luxury item rendered in sound. Those high-profile samples could easily cost $50,000, $100,000. Those without money get their creative options limited.

Even in today's litigious climate it's still possible to sample obvious sources, provided you give the results away for free. DJ Danger Mouse's Jay Z vs. the Beatles mashups and Girl Talk's pop-concentrate megamixes took this route to great acclaim. Sampling ultra-obscure (or merely non-Western) records brought commercial success to DJ Shadow and others. The rub is that these practices don't allow for any of the nuanced communitarian gravity that powered Public Enemy. On top of that, lots of sharing platforms preemptively block uploaded content when their algorithmic sniffers catch a whiff of what might be an uncleared sample. Every few weeks someone will tell me about how SoundCloud suddenly took down a remix of theirs without warning. If sampling is a historical-cultural conversation, increasingly you need a lot of money to join in.

CONTROL+X

What lawyers didn't kill off, metaphors did.

At the start of the 1990s, fewer than half of Americans used a computer at home or at work. By 2014 that number had leaped to 80 percent. One side effect of this spread is that the punching-up potential of cut and paste became harder to imagine as the language used to describe it got redirected into mundane software tasks.

Copy, *cut*, and *paste* downgraded to become the default operations we all use to push data around on the screen. Boring. Tidy. Toothless. Forget about reaching into the governing logic to fuck things up, dada-style. Any antiauthoritarian gestures made possible by the *cut* vanished with Ctrl+X. The hope that *paste* could forge unforeseeable links, creating unauthorized spaces of communication, got swept away by Ctrl+V. Social media demands sealed the deal: to manifest yourself online you must update your channels constantly, and the easiest way to do that is by copying and pasting info—now called *sharing* an article, *retweeting* an aphorism, etc., always on corporate media platforms.

This is readily seen in the glut of remix websites and apps. They each present a few songs or video clips, along with a small range of things you can to do "remix" them, such as activating a simple effect on a track or turning a loop on or off. The most recent one I crossed paths with is Al Jazeera's Palestine Remix project. I learned a lot from reading their FAQ. Some excerpts:

1. *What is a Remix?*
   A Remix is a piece of media that has been altered from its original form by adding, removing and/or changing its order.

3. *How can I make a Remix?*
   It's very easy. Search for anything that interests you. Find the scene you want. Drag and drop into the online video editor. Start adding scenes from dozens of films, and end up with your own creation. Note: So far the Remix tool doesn't work on mobile phones and tablets.

4. *How can I share a Remix?*
   Once you have made your own Remix, give it a title and click Share. Choose from the options available (Facebook, Twitter, Google+ or email). If you would like to save your project and work more on it later, just copy and paste the link that appears when you click Share.

6. *Can I add some other, external footage, music or voice-over?*
    No—however, you can add title or text between the different segments of documentaries.

7. *Can I download my Remix?*
    No. You can only save and share the link.

On it goes. The website's menu choices include Maps, Contact Us, About, Destroyed Villages, Definitions, Drone Footage, Quizzes, and Start Remixing.

Geopolitics? *It's a mashup!*

Palestine Remix's slogan reveals a lot: "You can tell the story too." You can't tell *your* story, you can't even tell *a* story; what you can tell is *their* story, using content licensed from the Qatari-government-owned news network, while the question of who might then see what you create goes unasked.

Al Jazeera's Palestine Remix, like its fellow remix platforms, is predicated on top-down control. You can't add your own footage or music, and you can't keep what you create, not even for personal use. We're encouraged to push the pieces of culture around more than ever, yet it's happening in a closed, airless system.

Twentieth-century cut and paste folded new territories into our maps. It worked to break up a monopoly of the imagination. The oppositional spirit of collage exists whenever edgy new expressive space is created. Things turn edgy when borders get crossed and the dominant organizational scheme breaks down. Alternative ways of being creep into the cracks. When what gets cut and pasted are simple pieces of data inside software environments, all the movement—the edginess—gets placed into specific con-tainers. *Can I download my Remix? No. You can only save and share the link.* The technique flattens, as it is turned into style and noth-ing more. There's no reaching across drastically different categories.

The constraining nature of such remix platforms makes it easier to see how the idea of remix as a hip or emancipatory gesture has lost all credibility. Sure, different versions of songs are nice: we've got choices. But when musicians or artists babble on about the power of remix, it's a sure sign that they've run out of things to say. Identity online (whether a song or one's per-sona) is marvelously fluid and ever changing—just as the structures that define our days (housing, jobs, debt, and other non-remixable items) seem harder to hack than ever. Contemporary remixing implies exhaustion, as if to say, "Rearrange the leftovers, they're all you've got left." But the world is still young. Our relationship to the patterns rippling across society can be more than one of remix and nudge. The very heart of it can be thought anew.

MISSING IN ACTION

Taking a look at the work of British Tamil musician Mathangi "M.I.A." Arulpragasam can help explain cut and paste's digital turn away from edginess and point to where the rambunctious media-crossing spirit may have gone. M.I.A. embodies a new kind of multiplatform artist: one who combines music, activism, and provocation with a deep understanding of how messages and style migrate across our increasingly wired mediascape. Born in

1975, she often references the revolutionary promise of early hip-hop, and her work hit the zeitgeist when cut and paste's new meaning was rebooting across our screens and minds in the 2000s.

"Who would've thought that a refugee from Sri Lanka would be influenced by Chuck D?" she mused in her first cover article. "I can't play and sing, but I'm gonna do something you could never copy and do. That's the philosophy of M.I.A.—cut and paste and bish and bosh."

In 2002, M.I.A. was a twenty-seven-year-old art school grad working in London's fashion industry. On vacation in the Caribbean, encouraged by musician friends, she recorded a few stripped-down beats using a $100 drum machine and scribbled out some lyrics. Back home, shy about her own talents as a vocalist, Arulpragasam auditioned several professional singers to perform her rhymes. None of them could express the sing-song chorus—"galang a langa a lang"—with quite the sparkle Arulpragasam had in mind, so she recorded it herself. Pitched between strident and childish, Arulpragasam's nursery-rhyme delivery perfectly complemented the dense, distorted backing beat that borrowed from the funk carioca music of Rio de Janeiro's favelas, splicing it at odd angles with Jamaican dancehall and electropop.

In the months to come she scrapped together a few more songs. A small label pressed the results on vinyl: five hundred copies. The debut M.I.A. 12-inch (2003) served as a template for all her music to come: agit-pop jingles informed by equal parts hip-hop, EDM, and indie rock, packed with in-the-know stylistic allusions to underground dance music from around the world.

She made sure tastemaker DJs received a copy; MP3s multiplied online. The results were brilliant: M.I.A.'s sassy bricolage trumped her admittedly limited vocal range. Catchy refrains and twitchy, bass-heavy beats kept things moving alongside lyrics that celebrated the cultural pileup of life in a big city.

A year prior to her first album's commercial release, M.I.A.'s free *Piracy Funds Terrorism* mix (2004) blended vocals from the unreleased album with popular rap beats and samples from Prince, the Bangles, Eurythmics, and more. On the back of the CD, M.I.A. is credited with "Executive Mish-Mash." In a deft reversal of the norm, M.I.A. debuted her own work as a mashup. Within a few weeks, an L.A. designer, a London reggae guy, and a New York hip-hop industry insider all sent me copies of *Piracy Funds Terrorism*. M.I.A. had sliced across style lines to become the must-hear secret that everybody wanted to be the first to tell their friends about.

Music bloggers and college radio picked up on *Piracy Funds Terrorism*. Remixes sprang out of nowhere. In another remarkable departure from the music industry standard, before M.I.A. had made even a single public appearance, her first tracks had already been downloaded millions of times and had established a global fan base (her first show, at the Drake Hotel in Toronto in February 2005, was a sellout). M.I.A. needed the nascent blogs and corners of online fandom the way those newly formed communities needed a sound track and a star.

I remember when the promo copy of her debut 12-inch arrived in the mail because the center label didn't indicate playback speed. At 33 rpm, the backing instrumental felt too slow.

At 45, her voice seemed too high. Whoever the artist was, she was clearly doing her own thing: respect!

"Galang" transported the listener to a land where the sonic and social status quo have gone topsy-turvy. The endearingly brutish instrumental was constructed from fidgety atonal squelches that stood in the place of melody. Where are we? The clunking rhythm offered few clues.

M.I.A.'s pan-stylistic approach championed Afro-British-Caribbean musical styles while not being beholden to their conventions. In tacit acknowledgment of her geographic and genre slipperiness, she grounds herself with a hometown shout-out right off the bat: "London calling, speak the slang now / boys say wha, gwan girls, say wha," spoken in smooth counterpart to the beat. "London calling" invoked the famous Clash song and album of the same name, which in turn referenced the BBC World Radio's World War II station ID. Arulpragasam and Clash frontman Joe Strummer attended the same art school, and each sought to bring politics and pop music into a shared space, with plenty of Jamaican musical influence to boot. Twelve seconds into her debut single, M.I.A. made it clear that she's a postcolonial media broadcaster, happy to give us all orders. When the Queen's English gets swapped out in favor of patois, surely reparations can't be far away. M.I.A.'s best work shares this level of thick referentiality and unbridled sonic joy.

The power of collage goes beyond proving that the dominant image or narrative can be redirected: it also wreaks havoc on perspective. Multiple points of view piled up in Höch's photomontages; M.I.A. keeps the frames of reference decidedly plural with a potent mix of sound, slang, and image.

M.I.A.'s early work spoke intuitively to so many of us because its sound articulated the distinctly contemporary condition of identity as loose and lossy data reproducing unfaithfully between storage outposts and playback opportunities. M.I.A. dramatized what happens when that *cut and paste and bish and bosh* leave the analog world and extend across network spaces, missing in action between MP3 and fan buzz and polemic and GIF and video. Today's individual no longer lives in a place. She lives at a velocity. Part artist, part attitude, part methodology, M.I.A. flourishes in these staticky disjunctions. The Internet loved Mathangi Arulpragasam, in part, because she sounded like it.

In 2013, M.I.A. designed a collection for Versace, based on bootleg Versace designs. "The theme of counterfeits, of those that produce and sell them, has always been part of the culture of M.I.A.," she said. "When I was contacted by Versace, it seemed a great idea to invert the circle. Versace's designs have always been copied; now it's Versace that copies the copies, so those that copy must copy the copies. So this will continue."

It's a fun formulation for sure. Who doesn't get a smile out of seeing high-end fashion-house logos plastered on knockoff goods in street markets around the world? It flatters those who believe they can tell the difference between the genuine article and a rip-off; it lets the people who opt for $20 drag handbags feel as if they're beating the system; and above all it reinforces the allure of widely legible status symbols. The fact remains that M.I.A.'s Versace line was only available to those who could afford to pay £120 for leggings (the cheapest item on offer). Copy-the-copies was the style, luxury gear was the statement.

Musically, M.I.A.'s amazing, a powerful collage counter-force against pop mediocrity. Politically, her work is less effective. The video for her 2015 song "Borders" felt, well, borderline offensive: M.I.A. uses hundreds of anonymous brown men as a backdrop to messianic self-imagining. She walks on water; they wait, inert, in crowded boats. Clinging to a tall barbed-wire fence, M.I.A. is lit by a spotlight; the men flanking her are silhouetted in darkness. "Borders, what's up with that?" she sings. "Identities, what's up with that? Your privilege, what's up with that?" M.I.A. is the only one who makes eye contact with the camera. In sound and image, "Borders" sentimentalizes the refugees while treating them as props. How could this be politically useful? The fact that Arulpragasam and her family fled to London as refugees in 1986 doesn't make her maudlin portrayal of border crossers in the midst of a major European crisis any more palatable. This is a music video—entertainment. To praise or promote it as a political act does an enormous disservice to the countless individuals actively working to improve the material conditions of refugees.

WAYS TO CROSS THE BORDER

Money slips around the globe as quickly as music. Bodies don't have it so easy. Airports and national borders are where the edges come down, hard, and the regulation of movement is felt at its most brute level.

In 2006 the U.S. government rejected Arulpragasam's entrance visa application. Uncle Sam doesn't have to explain reasons for denied visas and didn't in her case, although post-9/11 restrictions and paperwork delays have made it substantially more difficult for foreign artists to come perform in the States. Via MySpace and interviews, she used the episode to launch valid criticism of American immigration policy while flaunting jet-set privilege at the same time. Can't enter the United States to record your album with Timbaland? No problem. M.I.A. went on to record in Australia, India, Trinidad, Jamaica, Liberia, and the United Kingdom. Pretty good consolation prizes. Arulpragasam was back stateside to perform in Williamsburg, Brooklyn, within a few months anyway.

To be global is to be merely inconvenienced by factors of geography and immigration law.

To be local is to have few options.

The people in the United States most affected by border politics are the 12 million or so undocumented individuals at constant risk of deportation. Music made by people for whom borders are divisively real has a lot to say to contemporary cut-and-paste culture.

A few months after M.I.A.'s visa issues, I hopped into a Brooklyn taxi en route to JFK for an overseas tour. I hadn't paid attention to the radio until a Mexican ballad lyric leaped out at me: "Yo no crucé la frontera, la frontera me cruzó." *I didn't cross the border, the border crossed me.* I was off to be patted down by TSA at that very moment, and although traveling while black means that my bags get searched nearly every trip, I've never been detained, never experienced real passport grief. My consistent "random" security screenings were, in effect, a First World Problem. These lyrics reminded me of that. The couplet summed up a complex situation with poetic economy. The political borders shifted in 1848 as a result of the Mexican-American War, and issues of immigration, bureaucracy, drug trafficking, and more have kept them pressurized as of late.

Borders cross (and double-cross!) people all the time. I'd been blockaded behind English: I was aware that this Mexican *norteño* music spun tales of braggadocio and heartbreak, but until I crossed my own language barrier and really listened, it had never occurred to me that there were heavy topical songs as well. This wake-up call was "Somos Mas Americanos" by supergroup Los Tigres del Norte.

I began frequenting the half dozen Mexican music shops near my apartment to learn more. Speaking Spanish gave me access to the Mexican city inside New York City, which some call Puebla York in honor of all the immigrants from Mexico's state of Puebla. We enter the hidden city by listening, not looking, by staying still, not traveling. *Norteño* ballads were just the beginning. A wealth of geopolitically astute pop music was happening right under my nose in New York City. What tugged at my ear most insistently was the local take on cumbia, an under-the-radar phenomenon that points to what a twenty-first-century network-savvy cut and paste could be.

———

According to one legend, cumbia began when Colombian na-
tives and black slaves found accordions washed onshore from a
German shipwreck. The folk style crept into mainstream popularity in Colombia nearly one hundred years ago. By the fifties
cumbia colombiana had swelled into dapper big-band *orquestas*.
Currents of migration and chance spread cumbia outward to
everywhere from neighboring Panama to distant Buenos Aires.
For decades cumbia has subdivided, quietly becoming one of
Latin America's most popular styles, inspiring everyone from
Manu Chao to Calle 13. One of the great pleasures of listening
to cumbia is that it takes root differently in each region, since
no mainstream star has ever quite been capable of exerting stylistic gravity on all the satellites at once. Cumbia's deceptively
simple sound mutates everywhere it goes.

Its hallmark is an unhurried 4/4 groove built around low
drums and raspy shakers in a distinctive slow-train pattern.
Cumbia has no need for mellifluous ballad singers or show-offy
instrumental solos. Its steady sound packs enough swing to
keep the hips enchanted while remaining musically unpretentious.
You can dance to cumbia all night—even after working all day.

Depending on the place, the classic minor-key accordion
melodies may now be played on guitar, flutes, or synths (cumbia's
not dogmatic). Old and new singers alike love to shout,
"Cuuuuumbiiaaa," distending their syllables the way the genre
stretches meaning. Some view cumbia's tropical skank as the
missing link between upbeat salsa flash and the dubwise lan-
guor of reggae.

In Mexico, one of its biggest markets, cumbia can refer to everything from boy-band cheese to the slo-mo psychedelia of *cumbias rebajadas*, whose practitioners had been down-pitching cumbia records a good three decades before DJ Screw brought the same lazy-genius procedure to Houston rap. The branch known as *cumbia sonidera* (sound-system cumbia) began in Mexico City, where neighborhood sound-system operators prize rare cuts from old LPs. In Brooklyn shops I discovered the city's homegrown take on *cumbia sonidera*, whose rise has gone hand in hand with the surge in immigration over the last two decades.

Most of the other Mexican music popular in New York hews to the ballad form. In contrast, *cumbia sonidera* songs say little. The genre does not attract talented singers; when singing appears, it is often out of tune or comprised of amateurish lyrics discussing how wonderful cumbia is. If a cumbia (the word is used for the genre and also for individual songs) features a few stanzas of singing that tell some kind of story, that's often a flag letting you know that it's been imported from a hit in another genre, usually salsa.

Out of all the electronic music I listen to, it's hardest to identify in what years these NYC cumbias were made. Despite keyboards and samples, there's none of the emphasis on new sounds and production techniques common to electronic music, sounds that later double as time stamps. The producers aren't interested in cutting-edge audio or keeping in touch with outside trends. Neither novelty nor narration are particularly important.

Music that doesn't change is free to do other things.

A dozen or so *sonidero* parties dot outer-borough New York each weekend, with more rippling into New Jersey, Maryland, Virginia, and beyond. They range from family affairs such as *quinceañeras* (sweet fifteens) to blowout events at established Latin nightclubs, advertised with glossy poster campaigns— you can spot them by the blocky, cartoonish (think *Transform- ers*) *sonidero* logos. My favorite spaces to see cumbia are the odd in-between sites. The first *sonidero* party I attended was held in one such spot, an athletic center moonlighting as underground club, one block away from the dollar-a-dance dive bars and porn shops that populate this grimy south-Brooklyn zone under- neath the raised highway known as the BQE.

The only indication that something was happening was the Dominican security guard stationed out front. Inside, motor- ized lasers and spotlights emblazoned with *sonidero* logos cut through the fog machine's haze. The low-budget effects did their best to replace the gymnasium ambience with a spaceship rave vibe. A stage had been erected at the far end of a basketball court. At the other end soda and beer got sold out of ice-filled trash cans. No fuss. Beside them lay dozens of stacked plastic chairs. People took these as needed, arranging themselves in ca- sual rows on either side of the dance floor/court. The *sonidero* (soundman) stood over a stack of CD players and F/X boxes tucked inconspicuously next to the chairs.

For a *sonidero* to shine, he—almost always a he, unfortunately—must combine the selection and pacing skills of a DJ with a compelling vocal delivery style worthy of a popular radio host. Because a good *sonidero* never stops talking. His amplified voice booms out over the music, telling us about the song that's playing, about the song that's going to play, improvising odes to the classy beauty of the women at the dance, exhorting wallflowers to get their butts in action. Most of all, *sonideros* talk about who's at the event and who is elsewhere, on the other side of the border, or in another U.S. city.

Sonideros accept shout-out requests from the audience; these brief messages to family, friends, or lovers are scrawled to him on slips of paper or sent via cell-phone texts. The *sonidero* will notch down the volume of the song to call out messages atop it. Stuff like: "A cumbia with lots of rhythm and feeling . . . Listen! . . . We wanna see the dance floor full . . . Shout-out to the Aguila brothers, because they came here from Brooklyn! . . . The Fifth Avenue crew: Cricket, Spider, Chimo, Apache Maguey, the Thirteenth Cat . . . Aunt Linda in Georgia, I see you!"

The shout-outs may sound slight, yet they convey so much: *I see you, I'm thinking of you, I'd like everyone joined in this celebration to hear your name.*

What makes the scene so striking isn't the music per se; it is how the music explicitly gives voice to the social web that creates it and sets the sound in motion. The dances get recorded as audio or video, and these recordings are quickly made available for purchase. People buy them to remember or to send to those they've had shouted out. *Cumbia sonidera* recordings lie somewhere between memento and transmission. This sent me scratching my head when I first started frequenting Mexican music stores because I was looking for cumbia CDs that had individual tracks I could DJ. The last thing I wanted was re-cordings of a party, mic chatter and all. It's a positively baroque way to deliver a shout-out. I found it difficult to listen to (and impossible to DJ with). I still do. Yet the live *sonidero* albums are New York City's bestselling cumbia items, far outstripping the sale of CDs *without* some guy talking nonstop over the music.

Alejandro Aviles is one such guy. If you passed this short, humble man on the street, you would not notice. He's just a regu-lar dude, and the everyman aspect continues, with the same inconspicuous clothes and appearance, when he's manning the controls at a thousand-person dance party. Documented or not, migrant Mexicans face a peculiar invisibility in America: touted as bogeymen by anti-immigration conservatives, toiling long hours largely unseen in such places as farms and restaurants, where they make up more than half the working population. *Cumbia sonidera* is for precisely these people. As the master-mind behind Sonido Kumbala with more than two decades of experience in NYC under his belt, Aviles's voice is one of the most respected among East Coast cumbia fans.

"I was one of the first in line to criticize this world!" he told me at a café near his apartment in Queens. "I used to say that the *sonideros* talked too much, that they didn't let you listen to the song. I've had to eat those words. It's difficult because there are people who really criticize the world of the *sonideros* because they don't know it. But I can assure you, when they get to know it, they fall in love one hundred percent of the time. I know because it happened to me."

Why go through the trouble of attending an expensive dance, making a request, buying a recording of that specific night, then sending that chunk of audio data through snail mail or tucked into the luggage of a friend of a friend going to visit? Why don't you just facebook that hello, or better yet, call the person up? Why not send an e-mail? A text message even?

The beautiful inefficiency with which a *cumbia sonidera saludo* (shout-out) makes its way in the world deepens the import of the messages it contains. Bound up in the transmission is the beauty of acknowledgment: your name was sounded out at this party in Queens, your absence was noted, a few kind words to you were witnessed by the crowd, atop the music. Airing personal messages this way reminds us that these stories of distance and love tap into a shared condition familiar to every immigrant.

Cumbia sonidera in New York is more than music: it is music enlivened by live narration and audience-generated *saludos*, wrapped up in layers of recording and transmission. The scene threads together parties and MP3s and scrawled notes and text messages and CD-Rs and postal services, and more. The network of party promoters, shop clerks selling the recordings, and fans: they're all required to get the word out. Every link matters. The system shuttles messages between friends, lovers, and families in such a way as to emphasize the specific human connections at each point at the same time as it strengthens those lines of transmission. *Cumbia sonidera neoyorquina* devirtualizes social networks. It is a form of organization, a migrant politics that recognizes and uplifts its constituency through sound.

As such, it doesn't make sense until you participate. If you've got nothing invested in it, you'll just hear a lot of music being interrupted by a lot of talking. But if you've got something riding on the messages being relayed, a *sonidero* party turns into one of the most elaborate public listening environments out there. The *sonidero*'s patter swerves between improvised commentary, general crowd-hyping, and the act of naming with all the primal power that brings—plus the music, whose structural simplicity undergirds the nonstop stream of verbal information. The listener implied and created by all this is, to borrow a phrase from Jamaica's sound-system tradition, "broad—broader than Broadway."

All this creates a trusted media system. Inherent trust in the system doesn't come from technical protocols. Instead, the trust bubbles up from points of contact. Message creation, transmission, and reception must be tangible, human-legible at all times. It's a real peer-to-peer network. The music and messages circulate in ways that avoid gatekeepers—human and technical—outside of the working class Mexicans who are its core fans. This means keeping it small-scale, handmade. Even the CDs are burned in home batch burners. *Cumbia sonidera* sings in praise of the freedom to be found in small numbers. It reminds us that hyperconnectivity to a sea of strangers doesn't have to be every musician's goal.

To create a superstar would be against what *cumbia sonidera* believes in. To consolidate interest around a single figure would end the person-to-person communication that gives the music its social buoyancy. Regular attendees at *sonidero* parties don't even need to make a shout-out request—as soon as they're spotted, they'll get a *saludo* greeting. Affirm those present, sustain bonds across distance. *Cumbia sonidera* honors the humanity of its participants. It's a massive rethink about what a party can do.

And it all happens in the context of the relative invisibility of the Mexican working class in New York City. The people-powered media system sustains a counterpublic. For the undocumented or those facing other aspects of edge living, visibility can be a trap. *Cumbia sonidera* documents the undocumented—on their own terms. Not as individuals isolated by a hostile legal system or as anonymous, interchangeable workers, but as threads in a fabric patterned by song. The music never stops when the *sonidero* talks.

For those who believe in the power of community, the question of how to unite bodies scattered in space and time may be one of the most important issues music can explore answers to. *Cumbia sonidera* takes the condition of a real border seriously. Not as topic or backdrop, but literally, as a barrier around which communication and contact must flow.

Who would have thought that one of the most potent (if unassuming) grassroots communication networks was happening in rental gymnasiums under the BQE? Knots of cumbia fans scattered throughout La Unión Americana understand, for the shape and intensity of their connections are object lessons in how we can cobble together meaning on our own terms, in our own spaces, off-line and on.

Cut and paste. Or better yet, unstick and suture.

The slim hours of party are all too fleeting. *Cumbia sonidera* preserves the gathering's vitality by turning what would otherwise have been a flash-in-the-pan nightlife moment into a people-to-people network strung between borders. The ways in which the music circulates links those separated by work, by laws, by whichever of life's vicissitudes have befallen some of the least protected of this city's citizens.

Next time you're in a restaurant in New York—Thai, Italian, Ethiopian, vegan, French, doesn't matter (in this city well over a third of food-industry workers are undocumented workers from south of the border)—linger by the kitchen for a moment. Fair chance you'll hear cumbia wafting out. Unseen work, unseen celebration. The *sonidera* revolution grows far outside any spotlight. Not a fist in the air but a head down, in sight but out of notice, listening closely to what the lower frequencies have to say.

7

TOOLS

Is it worth it, let me work it
I put my thang down, flip it and reverse it
—MISSY ELLIOTT, "Work It"

Jimi Hendrix's father believed that left-handed guitar playing was a sign of the devil. So he forced his son to play right-handed. Righties hold the guitar neck in their left hand so as to leave the more dexterous picking work for their dominant hand. Lefty guitars exist, in less variety and with bigger price tags. When his dad wasn't around, Jimi would flip the guitar to play the same song with reversed hands on upside-down strings. He could tear through blues standards either way.

The father saw bedeviled talent. The son, christening himself Voodoo Child, reworked his instrument in defiance of what he was taught. Years later, when Hendrix could buy any guitar he wanted, he still preferred to hold a right-handed Fender Stratocaster guitar in the left-hand style and restring it in reverse order. The arrangement inverted the guitar body's acoustic design. The lower notes grew brighter and the higher notes sounded darker.

When you are not the person for whom a piece of technology is "user-friendly," you experience its limitations at a visceral level, so deep-seated that it can often feel as if *you* are the problem, not the thing into which you've been shoehorned. Being forced to play the "right" way helped Hendrix understand—and exploit—other, less visible systems affecting the instrument. His guitar heroics were merely one element plugged into a wider system involving the unpredictable circuitry of amplification, feedback, and studio trickery, all of it more important than reading staff notation, which he never bothered to learn. Within this matrix, the Fender didn't even get top billing: "I don't play guitar," Hendrix said, "I play amplifier."

Plug it in or flip it over to glimpse another world, or at least to get a feel for the arbitrary nature of whatever system's caught you in its grip. Then you can describe it, as Jimi did in his 1969 single "If 6 Was 9": "Now if 6 turned up to be 9 / I don't mind, I don't mind." Dramatic panning slammed his overdriven guitar into the left side of the stereo field and threw his voice on the right. They do not meet in the middle. There's no neutral ground. Where you stand matters.

Jimi Hendrix had been incorporating "The Star-Spangled Banner" into concert medleys for more than a year before his incendiary performance at the 1969 Woodstock Festival. Most of the festivalgoers had left by the time Hendrix took the stage at 9:00 a.m. on what was the fourth day of a three-day festival. (Hippies vs. clocks: the eternal battle.) He began by letting the opening notes of the anthem ring out, sustained and searing with distortion. The lone-guitar version seems odd, but not ironic. If anything, it is a stirring reminder of the way guitar overtones can make even individual notes fatten the air. After a scattering of melodic arabesques, Hendrix jagged "The Star-Spangled Banner" into a squall of gut-wrenching noise. For the next few minutes his playing took on the qualities of fire: elemental and hypnotic, edging in and out of control. Homage intersected iconoclasm as the anthem convulsed into moments of radical improvisation. Near the end, he quoted the mournful bugle call "Taps," a military song associated with funerals since the Civil War, and with dusk before that.

Was his playing sublime or sloppy? *The New York Times* wrote the whole thing off as "disappointing." Many turned to sonic realism to make sense of Hendrix's shattered anthem, claiming that the former army man was using his guitar to emulate the sounds of armed conflict, mimicking "the rockets' red glare, the bombs bursting in air," as an indictment of the American war in Vietnam.

To right-wing pundits Hendrix committed the sonic equivalent of dragging a flag through the mud. They interpreted his departure from tradition as sacrilege, unpatriotic. On the other side of the political spectrum, people interpreted his engagement through the lens of the Civil Rights Movement: Hendrix's anthem understood as a parable of personhood, the sonic enactment of a black American staking out a piece of the nation for himself.

The widely debated performance reached iconic status when the Woodstock documentary film hit theaters the following year. The intensity of the discussion shows just how unsettling Hendrix's version was. It divided the audience into individuals rather than urging them toward some easy consensus. For all its wild unresolve, I hear this as a song about responsibility and how to share it. Hendrix reconfigured "The Star-Spangled Banner" into a complex event in which each listener had to interpret this dalliance between noise and structure (or between sacrilege and respect) in order to establish his or her own meaning. By playing "The Star-Spangled Banner" irresponsibly, Jimi Hendrix handed the responsibility for its interpretation to each listener. Expressive freedom for himself, interpretive freedom for everyone else. Where one drew the line said more about the listener than it did Hendrix. Liberty lies in deciding. You are what you hear.

National anthems (played the expected way), protest songs, and chants at a rally all boil down to the same thing: sonic social glue. They seek to unite people around a shared sentiment.

Woodstock set lists were crowded with protest songs such as John Lennon's "Give Peace a Chance," released a month before. From the musically straightforward chords and the catchy group chorus of "All we are saying is give peace a chance" to the folksy guitar-and-tambourine production, recorded in the hotel room where Lennon and Yoko Ono were staging a "bed-in" while hosting famous friends and journalists, the single was engineered to be a sing-along anthem. The marketing was impeccable: more than half a million people sang it in unison at the Vietnam Moratorium march in front of the White House that fall.

Most music is doggish—it comes to you wagging its tail, unself-consciously hoping for you to like it. Hendrix's "Star-Spangled Banner" was feline, animated by a feral grace uninterested in reassurance or agreement as such. Despite the peace talk in his interviews and his own songs with antiwar lyrics such as "Machine Gun," Hendrix's ode to disunity lies a world apart from the anthem tradition.

Who can speak for a country? Politicians and the anthems they appropriate or antiwar protesters armed with sing-alongs? What about this poor kid from Seattle turned infantryman turned guitar god, black magic or white giving way to a purple haze: Can *he* sing the song of a nation? There's no yea or nay here; Hendrix sidestepped the very idea of authority to do something even better. He turned an anthem into a riddle.

"We do use electric guitars. Everything is electrified nowadays," said Hendrix in his first TV interview after Woodstock.

"So therefore the belief comes through the electricity to the people. That's why we play so loud."

The first international gathering to share ideas about the relationship between musical tools, cultural identity, and what it might mean to be modern happened in Egypt. At the urging of a French baron, King Fuad I convened the 1932 Cairo Congress of Arab Music, with the stated aim of "reviving and systematizing Arab music so that it will rise upon an artistic foundation, as did Western music earlier."

Phonographs and radios had made overseas music widely available in the Middle East, bringing with it palpable risk that Western influence would dilute the uniqueness of Arab music. The piano, with its eighty-eight tyrannically fixed keys, so at odds with the suppleness and profusion of Eastern tunings, had already made headway into well-heeled parlors across Egyptian high society, spreading European scales and songs. Developments such as these threatened to condemn music from this part of the world to a second-class status—and what were the defining characteristics of Arab music, anyway?

The three-week event dedicated to these issues drew luminaries from throughout the Middle East, as well as European musicologists and composers such as Béla Bartók. Eight committees convened to evaluate how Arab music could "evolve" (a popular term in the discussions) by such means as recording folk and classical repertoire, deciding upon fixed musical scales and notation methods, researching the "appropriateness" of various musical instruments, and formalizing music education.

Meeting notes reveal cross-cultural topsy-turvy. The Arab delegates, influenced by nineteenth-century European notions of progress, tended to regard their own music as inferior to that of the West, and so embraced sophisticated urban music as the site of greatest interest, whereas the European contingent was dominated by comparative musicologists who were trained to treat genre nonhierarchically, leading them to emphasize what they perceived as "authentic" Middle Eastern music—particularly the rural stuff—the further from Western influence the better. The ideological schisms proved so strange that the contemporary ear has difficulty not hearing sarcasm in statements such as this one, from a speech given to the Musical Instruments Committee by Muhammad Fathi in favor of piano adoption: "You should not judge our music on the basis of its present condition. If you find in it faults here and there, the flaw is not in our music but in most of those who work with it and in the dire need for true study in both artistic and scientific respects, and in this realm, you honorable Western gentlemen can offer us the greatest service."

The Congress raised profound, even troubling questions. More than music was at stake. To debate them was to probe issues at the heart of regional, national, even spiritual identity. Along with the committee meetings there were concerts and recording sessions, public addresses and newspaper articles. Informal talks spilled over into Cairo's cafés.

The cello, this newfangled import, should it be allowed in Arabic music? Should we abolish quarter-tone tuning to replace it with simpler European scales? The debate around harmony grew heated. Think of the Beach Boys or barbershop quartets stacking notes on top of each other to create thick, sweet layers: that's harmony. A distinctly European confection. It set Cairo Congress attendees wondering, *How much harmony is too much?*

At the same time, what curious musician wouldn't be intoxicated by access to exotic instruments such as the cello and electric guitar! There were new song forms, thrilling foreign theories on how notes should behave with one another—how not to integrate (or at least appraise and reject).

The Congress generated loads of discussion—and little agreement. The Committee for the Musical Scale arrived at the conclusion that there was simply no shared theoretical or practical basis to determine how one might divvy up a scale. The Musical Instrument Committee dissed the cello ("excessive pathos and sentimentality as well as . . . domineering"); people kept fighting about pianos. Broadly speaking, the Europeans argued for slow, internal change, while the Arabs wanted to reboot their musical heritage via an injection of Western tools. As for the audio recordings, the lion's share ended up in Paris and Berlin.

Ultimately the 1932 Cairo Congress (and smaller subsequent editions) failed to have an impact on the course of Arabic music as the king and his advisers had hoped. Hobbled by internal dissent, their high-level advising only managed to influence Egyptian music teaching and radio programming. For the most part, history had other plans. Indeed, the most influential Western voices, apart from Bartók's, were those of prominent German Jewish ethnomusicologists from Berlin; nearly all of them would be forced into exile the following year when the Nazis rose to power.

The Congress fascinates me because the basic issues about technological adoption and cultural adaptation remain timely. Digital tools callous our thinking as much as the analog ones ever did our hands, and their creative use and abuse can still enable artistic expressions that speak to national identity. From dervish analog energies conjured up on Woodstock amps to the electronic music tools of today, the beliefs of which Hendrix spoke take increasingly immaterial routes to reach the people. Nowadays to assert the changes the Cairo Congress organizers wanted, all they'd have to do would be to take over a few music software companies.

FRUITYLOOPS

Since time immemorial, people have crafted acoustic instruments in an astonishing variety of forms. In Werner Herzog's documentary *Cave of Forgotten Dreams*, a German pipes out "The Star-Spangled Banner" on a replica of a forty-thousand-year-old vulture-bone flute. The Basque *txalaparta* is fashioned from a tree trunk and must be played by two percussionists at once. Harps, tubas, church organs—they're all so strange! The overwhelming diversity reminds us that there's no final say on what music is or how one might manifest it.

Digital tools, on the other hand, shrink us down to a small set of options. Virtually all music software is made in the

United States or Europe. These programs all tend to do the same thing, in varying amounts, and that thing defaults to a narrow concept of what music can or should be. It matters because more and more music is being made using this tiny number of systems. Software tools are never neutral. They reinforce their builders' blind spots and biases and, once widely distributed, play an active role in maintaining those assumptions.

Throughout my travels, one piece of software pops up more often than the rest. Professional studios gravitate toward programs such as Logic and Pro Tools, and Ableton Live dominates the market for onstage performance, but out there in the muddy trenches of informal music creation, FruityLoops is everywhere.

"When FL appeared, most (but not all) other tools required owning hardware to even just make sound," its Belgian inventor, Didier Dambrin, explained to me over e-mail. "That has changed, but that may have helped making FL popular in places where it wasn't easy to get specialized hardware. And perhaps it's also easier to install." He's referring to how Fruity comes preloaded with drum-machine sounds and virtual instruments—and how other software, especially in the 1990s, didn't prioritize that out-of-the-box usability.

FruityLoops debuted in 1997. Before long, legal attention from the cereal company prompted them to change the name to FL Studio, although the original title persists among its users, often abbreviated to Fruity. The relatively simple interface welcomed first-time users. Sweetening the deal, Fruity ran fine on computers that might trip up on a bigger music app.

People liked FruityLoops. A lot. People who couldn't afford studios or instrument lessons (or didn't want them) could coax an idea into form while the inspiration lingered. Newbies were able to sketch out a rough song in minutes, then copy/paste in quick variations. All this proved particularly handy to kids who'd grabbed pirated versions without instruction manuals or couldn't read the language(s) they were written in.

Listeners familiar with the software will recognize its stock sounds liberally used in reggaeton, rap, and techno. Many of the highest-paid DJs and EDM musicians, such as Avicii, Afrojack, and Deadmau5, produce with FruityLoops. It's safe to say that FL Studio *is* digital music-making across sizable chunks of the planet.

Twenty years before Fruity, a British fanzine summarized the do-it-yourself ethos with a guitar diagram captioned "This is a chord. This is another. This is a third. Now form a band." Inexpensive computers running FruityLoops are the electric guitar and three-chord song of our time. They let urgency take form, clearing the path for a democratic roar of creation. Brilliant supernovas of expression such as Egyptian festival can result.

In bedroom studios across the world, FruityLoops and similar programs pass as an unquestioned default. If you want to make music, then these are the tools you use. End of story. If your music can't be created with them, tough luck. The software can be pushed beyond its limits, sure, but that requires a fair amount of know-how. The ability to work with decent, commercial-quality sounds from the get-go can make musicians less inclined to creatively mess it up. And more musicians don't mind using the exact same sounds as everybody else: Souljah Boy Tell 'Em's breakout hit, "Crank That (Souljah Boy)," was entirely Fruity presets. He opened up the software, clicked out patterns on a grid, and that was that—no adjustments to the sounds themselves. "Crank That" was perhaps the least personalized hit song in the last ten years. It's not just the sample packs and synths, either: standing behind preset sounds are preset ideas about how music should be made.

The software gives access, but it also exacerbates sameness. As Marshall McLuhan warned a half century ago, with media systems "every extension is also an amputation." The features that propel Fruity's global adoption simultaneously consolidate the type of music being produced and make it more difficult for other, less computer-friendly music to survive the transition to digital.

I reached out to Morganics, the Australian hip-hop educator who produced "Down River," the aboriginal rap song by Wilcannia Mob that got rebranded by M.I.A. "There's nothing worse than traveling from Brooklyn to Tanzania to see young kids making beats with the same sample pack on FruityLoops," he told me. "I want to hear local music, local sound, local accents, local slang, language, and issues. No need for mimicry of mainstream crap; let's celebrate what's unique and special about each place in the form of a song."

Take polyrhythms. Lots of non-Western music relies on them. They occur when two or more irreducibly distinct rhythmic points of view (points of hear?) coexist within a single song. That's how I'd describe the phenomenon—others might use a totally different framework to explain polyrhythms, and this plurality of understandings is part of what makes them so stubbornly human, and so resistant to digital encoding. Which is precisely the magic. Computers can't handle paradox or ambiguity, and polyrhythms are built from the stuff. Their notoriously subjective take on time and pattern exists smack in the middle of one of music software's many blind spots. Polyrhythms spring from an understanding of music, if not life itself, as shifting relationships of patterns, each with its own internal logic and timing.

So we're faced with a structure that forms the backbone to so much delightful music, especially in sub-Saharan Africa, that is illegible to the machinery. The closest thing to polyrhythmic compatibility in music software is the notoriously unfunky technical work-arounds that aggressively measure out the beats, which may be fine for math majors, but not for people like me, since it's not at all how folks from those traditions conceive of it.

During my time in Cairo I went to see a *zar* session held in an intimate, no-frills performance space three blocks south of Tahrir Square. The tea was free and the beats were heavy. *Zar* is matriarchal ritual music from Nubia, and as I watched three women pound out interleaved patterns on a variety of frame drums, I understood how it is said to chase out malevolent spirits. Their drumming pivoted between complexity and simplicity, never quite resting in either end. The room's energy crystallized. When I focused on the drum line any individual woman played, I found it easy to follow, yet the sum total of interlocking parts left me wondrously confused: I couldn't count it out.

I looked around. The youngest person in the troupe was pushing fifty. Umm Sameh, Umm Hassan, and Nour El Sabah: these three women are some of the only people in Egypt keeping *zar* alive. Unlike with the "monorhythmic" *baladi* beat, whose FruityLoops compatibility made *mahraganat*'s beefy electronic beats possible, if one wanted to play *zar* digitally, there's no simple way to encode it. From the software's point of view, *zar* is invisible. If the *zar* tradition can't make the leap into the digital, it may simply vanish.

Of course, software could never replace *zar*'s subtleties; it's as much a culture as a musical genre. What software could do is spark a connection between what these woman create and what a younger, more wired generation could make of it. Software functions as an archive of what we want to be possible at any moment; wouldn't it be nice to see what happens when we try to get stuff like *zar* in there?

It's a tough sell: those good enough to code for money tend to do just that. Tech start-ups pay more than "Zar 2.0." But rich musical cultures sustain a different type of value. And this is why we need programmers from far-flung corners of the globe making digital instruments to share. To strike up intergenerational conversations. To think about what a digital environment that respects the wisdom bound up in *zar* would do differently. To give some of the incredibly varied methods people use to make music a fighting chance in our electrified present. To keep things culturally polyrhythmic.

The history of electronic music can be written as a history of misusing tools. Scratching records. The creative abuse of

Auto-Tune. One of house music's most iconic and alien sounds is the "acid" squiggle, a slithery earworm that leaps out of a Roland 303 drum machine pushed beyond its limits. The examples are endless. So I admit, part of the reason why I want to see traditions such as *zar* get translated into the digital, however impressionistically, is so that other people can wield those tools incorrectly and blow our minds. More forks in the road, more left-handed turns. Give me new ways to be wrong.

SUFI PLUG INS

I came of age in the nineties, when experimental DJing was all the rage and live laptop performances were starting to happen. Electronic music presented me with seemingly boundless options. This techno-optimism soured when I learned how easily sampling could go from celebration to hurtful kitsch.

When I first heard Jamaican voices sampled in mid-nineties jungle records, I interpreted it as a form of respect. It was a kind of homecoming when I found ecstatic splinters of rap or reggae records that I knew and loved embedded in these alien-yet-familiar import 12-inches from London. This was Paul Gilroy's notion of the Black Atlantic in action. The British academic approached history like a DJ, focusing on the edge-connecting "routes" of transatlantic black culture instead of stable motherland "roots." The intensely physical dance music put these ideas into motion, full blast.

By the late nineties jungle's creative ferment had settled down into the more polished genre of drum & bass—fewer samples, less anarchic production choices. At the same time, jungle's go-to beat-making techniques had spread. The samples that connected jungle to Black Atlantic bass culture now circulated ad infinitum across genres, often deployed by producers far from that world to connote empty aggression. Sampling can forge cultural links just as easily as it can sustain a stereotype, but increasingly I saw the latter. Toss in a clip of some Jamaican man shouting ("Murdah dem!" was a popular choice)—and voilà, an instant hard-core club track. Jerk seasoning with extra salt. Any edginess generated by those samples relied on clichéd associations of black masculinity with aggression.

The caricature of the violent, impulsive black male is a minor annoyance if it only happens in music. Getting harassed by cops on the sidewalk after a late gig in Madrid or New York, it was a whole other story. Both projected fantasies affected me—they were not unconnected.

After that epiphany about sampling's nasty side, I started taking note of all the uncomfortable power dynamics caught up in the technique. Say you're making a song and want to incorporate an Indian tabla drum. Either you can look for someone who plays the instrument, explain the project, and negotiate a price (if any—at least you have the talk). Or you can nick tabla sounds from the Web. The first route is long, but it involves two-way communication and an opportunity to learn. The second approach is easy: there's no accountability to slow things down, nothing to coax you outside your comfort zone. More and more I saw sampling used to maintain cultural distance. Naive at best, creepily segregationist at worst.

I was part of the problem. I'd made an album under the name Nettle, sampling heavily from North Africa and elsewhere. It was no longer acceptable to continue down that road. I wanted community, conversations, the squeal of a feedback loop. In 2003 I moved to Barcelona and decided to put these thoughts into practice by branching out from samples to work with *actual musicians*. (For a DJ, this seemed like a radical option at the time.)

It didn't take me long to find Abdelhak Rahal, a violinist from Fez, Morocco. I was delighted when I realized how compatible our approaches were. *He thinks like a DJ!* I thought, wowed by the deft ease with which Abdel stitched together musical quotations and tailored melodies to rhythms. To *certain* rhythms, that is. During our first session I presented him with a spare hiphop instrumental. Any MC could immediately and comfortably rap over the simple beat. Abdel listened carefully, then launched into a soaring violin line. It was gorgeous. You can't summon up lines like this without years of experience. I knew in that moment that I'd chosen the right guy. Yet his timing was amateurishly off. Somehow this highly skilled musician wasn't syncing up with my computer-steady 95 bpm, 4/4-time FruityLoops beat. Then it hit me: my beat was suffocatingly, unbelievably square to Abdel, steeped as he was in the robust rhythmic diversity of Maghrebi music. We may have thought similarly, yet our "default settings" were so far apart as to be almost incompatible.

Another issue popped up: my synths could not readily accommodate the quarter-tone notes that Abdel played. Quarter-tone notes lie in between the notes of common Western scales and give Arabic music some of its unique character. Finessing note tunings presents no problems for string instruments such as a violin (where finger placement determines pitch), yet my synths (or a piano) could not reproduce them without some time-consuming under-the-hood tweaks. For the first few years Nettle performed with a desktop computer onstage because the software work-arounds that I'd Rube Goldberged together were far too complicated for a laptop to run.

I didn't use software, I fought with it. I got a pretty good idea of what values the good programmers in Berlin and Silicon Valley believe are important. Their assumptions became my roadblocks. I kept a running wish list of what I wanted in my musical tools. I began to wonder about other musicians from traditions not represented in software. What concepts would they be most excited to bring into the digital?

The questions were too juicy to remain rhetorical.

While hosting my radio show at WFMU, I met Bill Bowen, a gifted percussionist and coder with the precise set of skills to help me realize what I had been thinking of ever since those early sessions with Abdel. Customized music software. With *my* presets and assumptions embedded. The kinds of things I could open up and immediately use in Nettle performances, without any need for all the work-arounds and reconfigurations I'd grown used to. As the project developed, I saw an opportunity—since we were devoting so much time to these oddball digital instruments, why not make them shareable with the public?

Not only was my software going to do different musical things, I wanted it to surprise. All those software blockages I'd first experienced working with Abdel? This was gonna push back. I didn't want more choices. I wanted fewer, better choices. I wanted the entire experience of using my software to give what musicians call a vibe. I could do that by incorporating different defaults, different assumptions, different blind spots. Virtually every software update claims some new features. Rather than focus on making new things possible, I wanted to rethink "old" things.

Several months and a small mountain of friend-debt later, *Sufi Plug Ins* were born. Plug-ins are small programs that run inside a larger one, like an app for a smartphone. This was a suite of them: seven music-making devices based on non-Western conceptions of sound. The project sat somewhere between art provocation and instrument.

Four of the *Sufi Plug Ins* are virtual keyboard synthesizers. You can play them as is (they sound just fine), or you can adjust the settings to sculpt an enormous range of sounds. However, their tuning system is hardwired to North African quarter-tone scales. You can play all sorts of amazing music on these scales, from Umm Kulthum classics to Emirati pop, but you can't use them to perform Beethoven or Rihanna.

The rest of the plug-ins include a clapping drum machine, an audio drone generator, and something called "Devotion." All the *Sufi Plug Ins* are clearly labeled—in the Moroccan Berber language Tamazigh, using a two-thousand-year-old script called Tifinagh. Its future-ancient characters resemble a sci-fi Korean. The idea was that by frustrating (slightly, poetically) the user, I'd encourage them to explore the software's sounds guided by their ears, with less focus on the numbers or language (music software loves numbers).

Most virtual music gear is grimly efficient, with relentlessly rectilinear boxes, rendered primarily in gunmetal grays and blues. A macho visual environment. These had to go in the other direction: colorful icons based on traditional Amazigh designs that would also make sense to someone familiar with software synthesizer layouts. Designer Rosten Woo did wonders here. I was interested in giving people a playful experience of interface frustration, turning the tables on "user-friendly tech."

There is some English, however: whenever you hover the mouse over a knob, button, or fader, a "roll-over" infotext pops up. Instead saying something literal such as "volume" or "pitch," a fragment of Sufi poetry from twelfth-century Persia to today will appear, such as this one: "Here eloquence can find no jewel but one, / That silence when the longed-for goal is won."

The roll-over poetry and project title were inspired by Khalid Bennaji, a Moroccan musician whom Abdel invited to join Nettle. As a Sufi, Khalid sees musical collaboration as an extension of his personal beliefs. When he jams with a jazz combo in the town in southern France where he lives, it's not fusion for its own sake, or for the sake of diversity, but more like Khalid's way of sharing his spiritual convictions by meeting in that secular space of music. The openness he brings to song is a way of life. Sufism in Morocco is often associated with rural shrines where beliefs rely on oral transmission. It's a world apart from the Koran's more general religious power, based on the standard text and centered in distant cities. While Sufism means many things to many people, one of the recurring concepts is an emphasis on direct personal experience over doctrinal teachings.

We live in a world where it is almost unthinkable that a tech product with global uptake could emerge from Africa. The farther one lives from tech hubs such as Silicon Valley or Redmond, Washington, the less likely that any gear or app will be made with your specific needs in mind. I wanted to flip that dynamic (on a shoestring budget): to encode digital tools for my small group of Berber friends in Casablanca and myself, then make those tools available to a global audience.

Sufi Plug Ins had to be free. Those familiar with code can open them up and mess with the innards. People always ask, "Why don't you charge money for them?" The idea of the gift at the heart of it was supremely important. Could a spirit of generosity be contagious? I hope so. Giving people stuff for free can be wonderfully disarming, like smiling at strangers in New York. Free meant no pressure to follow convention. I could make the plug-ins as weird as I wanted. How could anyone complain? There was no pressure to make the project more sellable. If I charged for them, then I'd have to provide customer support—to answer questions about how they work, which would have gone against their whole raison d'être. *Sufi Plug Ins* are what you make of them. My Berber friends can read the Tifinagh, happily surprised to see this strange bit of software in their native tongue. Kids elsewhere can experience the visual frustration/poetics. The longer you use the plug-ins, the more you start to recognize the Berber words. If anything, I hope they work as a gesture of noise and responsibility in the Hendrix sense.

Riddle and tool, provocation and dream. Why shouldn't software be able to be all these things at once? Since the first iteration of *Sufi Plug Ins* were custom-made to function inside my go-to program, Ableton Live, for the next step I want to translate them in a format called VST, which will enable them to be plugged into most music-software environments—FruityLoops included.

Inspiration for the final of the *Sufi Plug Ins* came when I was researching in Morocco. I was walking through the Casablanca medina when I chanced upon a lingerie/hijab/women's sportswear stand blasting Amazigh music with a handful of CDs for sale. The guy must have been pleased with my selection, because after I asked for a few albums from what he had on display, he pulled out a CD from behind the counter: *Imanaren*. It was extraordinary, blending together various styles of Berber music from south Morocco in a distinctly contemporary way, with spacey banjo lines and haunting group vocals. The beats were great too. Eventually I tracked down Hassan Wargui, the singer/songwriter for the group. He lived in Casablanca, and that medina stand was the only shop that carried the CD. *Imanaren*'s too noncommercial for other vendors to trifle with. Hassan and I became friends over the summer. When he mentioned that we should visit his village sometime, I leaped at the chance.

One week and a ten-hour night drive from Casablanca later, I was greeted by Issafen's striking landscape. Empty adobe houses crumbled back into the rocky hillside, and near them families live in newer self-built cinder-block palaces. The village lines a sliver of oasis green where date palms, figs, and monstrous olive trees have sprung up around a riverbed that's walkable barring flash floods.

A dozen years ago Issafen had no electricity. Power lines were strung when the new king came to power, and now Hassan and his buddies use cell phones to shoot YouTube shorts whose genre scramble is inspired by Bollywood's action-romance-comedy-melodrama-all-at-once attitude. The women still haul water up from the creek predawn, and down the road the cybercafé's sign has been around so long that it's nearly rusted out of legibility.

Hassan would love to return, but to make music he has to be in the city. His father, Abdellah Wargui, was kind and impish with us gawky strangers (despite the fact that my friends and I were eating him out of house and home). Yet he frowned upon music. So Abdellah had never heard any of his son's brilliant creations—some of the best in the country and the reason my friends and I had unceremoniously descended upon the Wargui family home in the first place.

Hassan's crew is not the first to have gone to the city looking for work and also for more creative license than the cave down by the river (their rehearsal space) provides them. It's not just about the music. If you live in the village, you live by village rules. No music and, said Hassan, no romance. Issafen's electricity generation swoons over Bollywood videos and cultivates a parallel fantasy life of whirlwind passions while families nudge them toward arranged marriages. From Casablanca's clamor you can feel nostalgic for the ways of the village; once you're actually there, you mostly just feel oppressed by them.

I went there thinking that I was taking a break from *Sufi Plug Ins*, which I'd been translating and scheming up in Casablanca. Issafen had a surprise for me. Our first day there, we heard a beautiful *azan* being sung to call the villagers to pray at the neighborhood mosque. The next day we learned that it was Abdellah Wargui. He recites Issafen's call-to-prayer daily, with a clear and powerful voice that was inherited by his son. Yet *Imanaren* had never been heard here.

The situation sent my head spinning.

I started to think: This Berber muezzin, who performs the call to prayer with such a melodious, joyful voice but frowns upon music—could *Sufi Plug Ins* respond to this particular situation?

A few months earlier I was buying CDs from a music stand in the main square of Marrakech when the *azan* sounded (unlike in Issafen, this one was prerecorded, as is increasingly the case). The clerk's hand shot out to the pause button on his stereo—but he wasn't playing any music. We looked at each other and laughed. The guy was so used to pausing his music during the call to prayer that it had become pure reflex.

That led to the answer: silence. The final of *Sufi Plug Ins*, "Devotion," lowers your computer's volume five times a day out of respect for the Muslim call to prayer. Presets include Agnostic, Fervent, Devout—Atheism is not an option. It's an homage to the Wargui family in Issafen, with a nod to Hendrix's notion that "the belief comes through the electricity to the people."

———

Less than twenty-four hours after I put *Sufi Plug Ins* online, a composer in Bahrain e-mailed me a bristling noise track he'd made using it. The notes for his score were generated, somehow, by a photo of a stray cat superimposed with a lot of circles and lines. He then had the *Sufi Plug Ins* synth tuned to his favorite Arabic scale (*hijaz*) play those wild-cat-sourced notes. It sounded like . . . chaos. I was thrilled. It was working. The tools were out in the wild, already helping people to create in ways I could never have imagined or programmed for.

DIGITAL VINYL

Tragedy led me to the tool that has most transformed my own performances.

The first year my gig schedule gave me more than a hundred nights on the road was 2002. Midway though a packed U.S. tour with Kid606, we were cruising in the slow lane on the highway outside Santa Fe, New Mexico. Even better than the balmy spring afternoon, it was a day off—there was no rush to get to some venue. So we took our time, anticipating a mellow hotel night when we could catch up on e-mails or simply enjoy the restorative quiet.

When our van driver noticed lights coming up directly behind us, fast, he thought nothing of it. Midlife-crisis sports cars speeding across highway lanes are a familiar sight, as is seeing those cars pulled over by state troopers. The highway was otherwise empty, and besides, we were in the slow lane.

But no. The fast-moving car didn't switch lanes. It smashed into the back of our van with a nightmarish crunch. The jolt sent us swerving wildly as our driver fought for control. Gear flew around, including heavy four-foot-tall speakers. It would have been disastrous if any of that stuff had fallen on *us*—I'd dozed off in the backseat. We were incredibly fortunate that the van didn't flip over.

Banged up but intact, we untangled ourselves from the mess and stepped onto the side of the road. The van was totaled. Its rear had crumpled inward, so at first it didn't look as if we'd lost any equipment. Then my heart fell. Everything was still inside—everything except my two pieces of luggage. They had flown out the shattered rear windows; each contained about fifty of my best records. A thousand-foot smear of vinyl fragments and torn-up record jackets littered the road behind us. Dazed, I wandered up and down that stretch of highway struggling to find an unbroken record. No dice. The highlights of years of collecting, pulverized by a drunk driver. Who was nowhere to be seen. A hit-and-run. When the cops showed up, they marveled that he (it must have been a he) was able to drive away at all.

Around this time the digital vinyl system (DVS) began looking attractive.

A handful of companies make them: Traktor Scratch, Serato, Virtual DJ, Ms Pinky, and more. They all let you use a regular turntable, DJ mixer, and vinyl record to spin MP3s. It looks and feels just like the traditional DJ setup. The special thing is the records themselves. They're normal audio records, yet the audio they have is piercing sine-wave whine, a "timecode" that the laptop listens to to interpret precisely where on the vinyl the needle is. So you drag an audio file into the program, drop the needle on the record, and the DVS will instantly play back the MP3 using the vinyl as controller. The software determines the needle's location, how fast it's moving, and whether it's going forward or backward, and applies that information to manipulate the MP3 playback accordingly. It may sound complicated but the magic of the system is listeners can't hear any difference, and more important, DJs using DVS can't feel any difference. It's sensitive enough to ensure that any spitfire back-and-forth vinyl-scratch trickery translates seamlessly. Want to switch songs? Drag and drop the file onto the DVS software and keep mixing. DVS augments but does not necessarily replace standard 12-inches: at the flip of a switch one can play the audio from a regular vinyl too.

When DVS first hit the scene, I was suspicious. *What'll people think when they see me onstage with a laptop next to the decks? What'll I think?* No matter what the technology, the being-in-the-moment of a live performance is magical. Interrupting that spell to stare at a glowing screen onstage is a drag for performer and audience alike.

I was also worried about latency. When saving documents or opening programs, the ultrabrief lag between when you tell the computer to do something and when it gets done is trivial. When performing with a virtual instrument, that latency can accumulate enough milliseconds to throw off one's timing. For musicians, timing is—*pregnant pause*—everything. Even casual listeners feel how a band member off by a sliver of a second can make the difference between a group's sounding together or sloppy. I feared that my DVS would have latency—or worse, that it'd freeze entirely. I'd dealt with audio software that crashed if you so much as looked at it the wrong way. Fine for studio but unacceptable during a gig.

Then I'd flash back to that stretch of pavement outside Santa Fe, and the benefits of DVS reasserted themselves. How could things get worse?

Even without highway accidents obliterating my collection, lugging around a third of my body weight in rare plastic for months at a time was a ridiculous labor of love. Or maybe just ridiculous. I was never interested in the so-called warmth of vinyl, or the geeky digger cred of owning rare slabs of wax. I love vinyl devotees who insist on DJing only with "real" records—but don't understand them. The more precious the record, the better it is to digitize it and keep it safe at home!

Before DVS, whenever I got a killer song on CD or an unreleased single from an artist that I absolutely had to incorporate into my DJ sets, I'd take a dollar van out to a Jamaican studio in Brooklyn to get a dubplate cut. Unlike vinyl, which must be mass-produced, dubplates are one-off records individually "cut" into discs of soft acetate. They cost me about $40 a pop. You can DJ them just like regular records, with the caveat that each time you play a dubplate, the record needle will sheer off some of the acetate, making it scratchier. After a few dozen spins they usually need to be retired. The rarity and cost made dubplates a point of pride among DJs. If you were packing dubplates, that was a sure sign that you took DJing seriously and had a grip of unreleased heat in your bag. DVS upended all that. The thought of being able to download a new MP3 and spin it out moments later using vinyl boggled my mind. Playing files off my laptop meant that I could have hundreds, thousands, of songs at my fingertips while ditching the backbreaking record crate. (Spoiler alert: my laptop now contains roughly two thousand songs expressly for my DJ sets. If that were vinyl, it'd weigh about 650 pounds.)

For the rest of that fateful tour I spent every spare moment hitting record stores in a desperate attempt to restock my depleted crates. As soon as I got home, I took the DVS plunge and never looked back. Scratch and Serato and their cousins made it so easy to cross that line because they zoom in on turntable and mixers as *interface*. It's not about sounding "better" or doing "more." It's about letting us continue to take advantage of all the expressive possibilities opened up by hands-on vinyl manipulation. The tech piggybacks atop the existing turntables and mixer setup that was so useful to me in the first place.

If I'd started DJing just a few years later, I may never even have touched turntables. I entered on the tail end of vinyl's reign as a performance tool. I always try out CDJs and other newer formats, yet the detail and sheer physicality of turntable-as-interface remains unparalleled. All the years I'd spent practicing on my Technics 1200s had developed into muscle memory. I don't have to think about what I'm doing, a sure sign of effective technology. DVS let me hold on to that physical, body-smart way of interacting with music. It's always fascinating when tools sink into the bodily unconscious; perhaps that's what handicraft is.

Once, on tour in France, I was flipping through Twitter a few hours before my show. Mexican producer/DJ Antonio "Toy Selectah" Hernández, announced that his laptop had been sto-len in Colombia. He asked for help recovering it, or at least some of the lost data. He too had a gig that night. Last time I'd seen him, we'd swapped music, so I was able to upload a hand-ful of the unreleased songs he'd given me, as well as some tunes that would prove useful to his set. Several other friends who had seen his Tweet did the same. Toy's laptop was never recov-ered, but he was able to perform that night.

I miss the subway–to–dollar van journey to cut dubplates in Brooklyn, but those days are over. More than once I've been e-mailed a brand-new tune while backstage and been able to in-corporate it into my mix minutes later.

DVS and *Sufi Plug Ins* are both a little bit out of time. They're children of the twenty-first century who lean into the future, yet they're agnostic about progress. Moving forward some-times means holding on.

8

LOOPS

A civilization comes to an end when a people no longer takes its own chronology seriously.

—ELIAS CANETTI, *Crowds and Power*

When *tribal* (tree-BALL) first started bubbling out of Mexico City around 2005, it was dubbed *tribal* pre-Hispanic, after local producer Ricardo Reyna's "La Danza Azteca," the first tune to pull pre-Colombian samples into tribal house. This is what *tribal* refers to—not the energetic percussion patterns of tribal house, but tribes: indigenous Mexican and "African," which the music evokes via clip-clopping drum grooves and twee melodies played on pre-Hispanic flutes. The genre morphed into *tribal guarachero* when innovators such as DJ Mouse started integrating elements of the slinky, groove-based style known as cumbia and Afro-Cuban traditions into their tribal house. *Guarachero* refs to the metal shaker that gives cumbia its telltale raspy shuffle. Hovering around the dance-all-night tempo of 130 bpm, the music's syncopated street bump blends well across the house-music spectrum.

In Mexico City's massive Zócalo plaza, which forms the new sound's mythic home, Indians play flutes and drums in Aztec costumes, spicing the city's unhealthy air with their burning frankincense. The nearby pirate marketplace of Tepito stocks countless low-bitrate *tribal* CD-Rs. Rewind five hundred years, before the Spanish arrived: Zócalo was the center of Tenochtitlán, the Aztec island metropolis that was one of the world's largest cities. Workers building a subway line in the 1970s found leftover pyramids. Tepito has been an active market since Aztec days too. "In Mexico," wrote novelist Carlos Fuentes, "all times are living, all pasts are present."

Architecturally, this present past is experienced as a layering: Zócalo's cathedral was erected from stones used in the Aztec temples that stood there first. In music those layers can be grasped all at once, and it becomes a simultaneity. *Tribal* agrees, churning out futuristic club bangers fed on hearty servings of ancient music.

I first heard of *tribal guarachero* in 2008, described as "the Mexican ghettotech . . . Very undeveloped yet" on a friend's blog post. Artwork on the 168-song MP3 CD showed "three indigenous face masks from different eras and a crowd at a rave." In theory, it was promising. In practice, the haphazardly assembled CD-R compilations available in Mexico City were mostly crappy-sounding tribal house MP3s with Eurotrance hits mixed in by the careless vendors. The only interesting thing about the few rudimentary *tribal* beats included was that they were there at all: these were clearly the sounds of amateurs struggling with software-based music production.

When next in Distrito Federal (also known as DF, pro-nounced "Day-Effay," as Mexicans refer to their capital), I asked around. Word on the street confirmed that the megalopolis's budding *tribal guarachero* scene had shared crowds and DJs with reggaeton, then faded away as reggaeton won out. This happens a lot in World Music 2.0. Wisps of styles float online or across a region, pausing to alight in someone's mixtape or blog write-up before they disappear for good. Sometimes a scene is simply two or three producers exploiting a common sample library for a few months, creating tracks that outsiders mistake for a movement. Journalists can make things worse by rushing to report on some nascent sound before it can resemble the premature hype, much less develop enough to withstand the pressures that accompany it. *Tribal* looked to be this.

Two years later I was invited to DJ in the northern Mexico outpost city of Monterrey. Antonio "Toy Selectah" Hernán-dez, one of my absolute favorite people to talk about music with, told me about a *tribal* rave for teens happening on Sunday after-noon that he wanted to drop by. These young *tribaleros* were in diapers back in 1996 when Toy's hip-hop group, Control Ma-chete, sold more than a half million copies of their debut album, yet it comes as no surprise that he was the first adult to cham-pion *tribal*. Toy slingshot his exposure with Control Machete into a lasting career in A&R and producing. He won a Grammy for his work with Puerto Rico's Calle 13 and has always remained on the cutting edge of Latin pop.

He'd been in touch with the scene's producers and reported back that the club's resident DJs, Sergio "Sheeqo Beat" Zavalas and Erick Rincón, were the best, most dedicated young guns of them all. I'd been disappointed by the bare-bones *tribal* MP3s I found in the capital, but when Toy's excited by something, you take note. I extended my stay to join him.

Never underestimate Mexico.

The weekly rave took place in the middle of downtown. A spill of revelers gathered at the venue's nondescript doors. Admission cost about $3 for boys, $2 for girls. Not all would make it inside: twin brothers in clown makeup sat on the curb, too poor to enter. A woman in a Saint Judas T-shirt sold loose cigarettes, amaranth bars, and tiny plastic-wrapped studs so the kids could customize their piercings before entering. The boys paid more attention (and money) to their hairdos and clothes than did the girls, who gravitated toward halter tops and hot pants—sexy/functional for the sticky, hundred-degree heat. Among the subcultures present were *los Texas*, Monterrey's take on the cholo style; *los fachas*, emos with a punky edge; *reggaetoneros* in oversize U.S. basketball jerseys; and more. The most wildstyle were *los Colombianos*, hood fashion visionaries who gel their hair into extravagant spiked sideburns with big patches shaved away, dressing baggy and colorful with suspenders, high-perched baseball caps, and generous amounts of Virgen de Guadalupe accessories. The "Colombians" exude gangsta Catholic manga vibes from a decidedly street perspective. While it had petered out in Mexico City, in Monterrey *tribal* didn't serve a niche audience; on the contrary, it provided a common banner for these scattered young tribes to unite under, just as the party gave them a space. We passed through metal detectors and a patdown to enter the cavernous club.

Inside ArcoIris (Club Rainbow), Sheeqo Beat spun first— no laptop or turntables, just CDJs. One of the *Harry Potter* movies was projected behind him, and the club's coed dance squad performed their coordinated acrobatic moves in front. You couldn't see the stage from entire wings of the club, but the party raged there too. Wildly unmodulated postpubescent sexuality and hyperkinetic adolescent energy reached new peaks with the *tribal* beats. There was no norm. A boy who couldn't have been more than nine was grinding with a girl nearly twice his size and age. The dancers' cages were open to all: they filled with a fearless range of body types, with everything being documented via cell-phone pics. Many kids don't have computers or regular Internet access, but everybody here sweats the photo-sharing Web service Fotolog, and its social network of "floggers." "It's the easiest way to get known in Monterrey," said Rincón. The Sunday parties provided extra incentive for people to upload photos of their looks and lives as a mad acceleration of fashion paralleling the evolving music.

Sheeqo tended toward percussion-heavy tracks. Rincón's set was more playful. Simple three-note bass lines (nicked from Mexican music that imported it from the nineteenth-century German population there) pumped along frisky drum patterns. The beat-heavy genre had gotten more synthy over the past few years, and Rincón's stated mission was to integrate synth melodies with his beloved cumbia and pre-Hispanic. Most of the music played was the DJs' own, and they mixed it energetically. While *tribal guarachero* has signature sounds, the party DJs stayed open: they took extended forays into reggaeton, some rap *en español*, or, at the right moment, a slowed-down *cumbia rebajada*. When they dropped reggaeton, they didn't play radio-ready summer tunes, though these are crowd-pleasers across Mexico. Instead the DJs spun reggaeton *beats*: dance-floor edits, chopped-up vocals. The bass/guitar lick from Chaka Demus & Pliers' reggae classic "Murder She Wrote" was the most common sample of the afternoon. From week to week DJs customize their original songs and remixes in a tight feedback loop of creativity.

It's hard to believe that the U.S. border lies only two hours away, but that's the magic of Monterrey, Mexico's richest city. Proximity to the United States keeps it looking outward. The city prides itself on a century of bustling industry, a long legacy of bringing raw materials from around the Americas, where they get transformed into exports and profits. Same thing happens with the music. The style that Mexico City pioneered, then discarded, was retooled in Monterrey. Four decades earlier, it happened with cumbia. In the seventies, cumbias from Colombia achieved such popularity in Monterrey that Colombian musicians emigrated to capitalize on their ardent and unlikely fan base. Before long, bands based in Monterrey branched into their own style of *cumbias colombianas*. ArcoIris DJs came to an abrupt halt at 8:00 p.m. to make room for precisely this homegrown bassy cumbia style, as performed by one of their city's most beloved "Colombian cumbia" bands, Javier Lopez y Sus Reyes Vallenatos. They brought down the house with versions of classics penned well before the audience was born.

Anywhere else on the planet, switching gears from DJs spinning that season's electronic club anthems to a seven-piece live band playing a style of music forged in the 1950s would kill the dance floor or at least split it in half. Here nobody batted an eye. If anything, the dancing intensified, shifting into a group swirl pattern used specifically for cumbia in this part of the country. "Look"—Rincón nudged me—"the band is a bunch of boys too!" It was true: bandleader Lopez had been in the game for decades, but most of his crew were just a few years older than the average ArcoIris patron. The youngsters responded to the intergenerational spread with an open-minded understanding that marked serious sophistication. The sense of legacy and place being communicated was stunning. Inspirational. Weirdly democratic too: the cultural commons where these songs and dances are stored is accessible by all.

I've spent time in music venues all over the world, from bacchanalian raves in Bristol to Egyptian street weddings. In each case I had some inkling of what was in store before I showed up. This extraordinary party caught me by surprise. The traces of *tribal* that made their way online and into Mexico City's markets couldn't convey the least bit how rich, how multilayered, how culturally active, the scene had become in Monterrey. I boarded a Monday-morning flight home with ringing ears. A month later I was back to report on what was happening for *Fader* magazine.

First stop: Rincón's home studio. He was sixteen years old. Level-headed and soft-spoken, the teenager radiated preternatural calm as he and some of his friends folded into a tiny studio in the back of his parents' Monterrey apartment. "I'm crazy!" interrupted one, who immediately started beatboxing. Rincón said, "I wasn't learning anything, so I dropped out of school two years ago." The young producer didn't own a microphone, but MCs came by anyhow. Rincón squinted at his computer screen through shaggy hair, wearing a Day-Glo T-shirt, skinny Smurf-colored jeans, and white Chuck Taylors. "What month is it?" He found his latest project files and booted up Fruity-Loops, then a pair of overworked PC speakers burst into life. A steady house kick drum got crosshatched by rootsy percussion swinging hard in a different time signature. Electro synths re-peated a staccato riff, but the bass line dreamed of Mexican tubas playing polka. Right before the track started to make sense, it downshifted into a cumbia break. In ArcoIris, this was the pre-cise moment when more than three thousand kids would scream and throw their hands into the air, but that afternoon Rincón was tweaking sample settings with sound libraries nabbed off *tribalero* chat rooms, prepping for the *quinceañera* he'd DJ later that night. His mother stuck her head in: "They get so into the music! Sometimes they don't leave this room, they just sleep on the floor."

A dozen years ago this music didn't exist. Today, *tribal guara-chero* sound-tracks tough Monterrey girls' *quinceañeras*. Rincón's cowboy brother skipped through northern Mexican tunes as he drove us to Royal Diamond function hall for the *quinceañera*. KFC, Starbucks, and cheesy Tex-Mex chains can all afford to keep signage blazing after closing hours, so illuminated logos of American brands dotted Monterrey's nightscape. But the only places to get food at this hour were bare-bulb taco stands, and those sparkling lights clustered in the hills marked rough barrios such as La Independencia, home to generations of cumbia followers and too-young foot soldiers manning the corners in knockoff Ed Hardy gear.

While the mainstream media's narrative for Monterrey tells of a formerly safe city ravaged by encroaching drug wars (it went from being one of the safest cities in Latin America to one of the most dangerous in a few years, with more than three hundred murders in the months surrounding my visit), *tribal guarachero*'s potency and exuberance tells the other story: irrepressible youth culture sweating it out in a healthy scene so hype that they barely have time to realize what's being created. Sunday afternoons at ArcoIris proved how a motley gathering of several thousand kids with few resources among them could create a world-class conflagration of sonic and fashion culture. The underage parties there walked a knife's edge between innocence and its loss. *Quinceañeras*, in turn, celebrate coming-of-age.

Security guards let us in. Wearing a skimpy electric-blue tutu, birthday girl Nalleley danced with her father as mariachis played "The Last Doll." Everybody knew the words, everybody knew the moves. As the live band hit its stride, their strummed guitars started to resemble sped-up *guaracha*, the scraper percussion rasping out cumbia's telltale shuffle. The more strands of Mexican music you hear, the more you'll catch structures and rhythms that *tribal guarachero* has cannibalized.

While *tribal guarachero* honors a reconstructed past, there is no nostalgic sentiment such as the one appealed to by touristic "Indian" moments throughout the country. It sidesteps Aztec kitsch, a very real category in Mexico.

The genre creates a space where kids can playfully experiment with how local roots—from *narcocorrido* drug ballads to Israeli psychedelic trance techno (they call it psycho) popularized by the rave scene—tangle with random Internet click-trails (inexplicably, *tribal* samples lots from Egyptian percussionist Hossam Ramzy). It also explains those persistent swinging triplet beats. The Monterrey kids grew up hearing *rancheras*, *huapangos*, and *corridos*, all in 3/4 time. This meter reappears in folk music across Latin America, and it creeps into *tribal* even though they're using software that defaults to 4/4 beat structures. Kids all over the world make tracks with FruityLoops software, but you have to be strong or stubborn to pack it so thick with structural references to other Mexican music—particularly folding in those alternate time signatures, those sneaky triplets that move the body more subtly. The Mexican time at the heart of *tribal* sets it apart from other more visible genres of World Music 2.0.

All this is why Toy was convinced that *tribal* would reach the rodeos, blue-collar bars, and related stomping grounds of

Mexican popular music (on either side of the border)—because it derives from straight-up unromantic Mexican dance music and taps into wider aspects of Mexican thought. *La gente del pueblo* will instantly hear its roots and understand where it's coming from, at the same time its influence from adjacent forms of EDM will keep things forward-looking.

Back in his studio after the ArcoIris party, Toy, one of those rare dudes who decorates astute observations with trucker-grade swears in English and *Español*, rhapsodized *tribal* as "a truly strange mental confusion" in Mexican youth culture: "The same person will be listening to psycho, Tiësto, Paul van Dyk, and Los Tucanes de Tijuana. That person will also be listening to pre-Hispanic drums and percussion from who knows where, saying, 'I don't know where these drums are from. I fucking love Santería and I don't understand it, but I'll use it. Plus I'm gonna put on some berimbau, though I don't know if it's from Brazil or what.' *Tribal guarachero* is catharsis, sonic catharsis."

As for *las fresas*, the snobby upper-class youth who sniff at populist Mexican culture, they'll get sucked in by *tribal*'s Internet-savvy sound, he claimed. Best of all—Toy thwacked my arm for emphasis—"the music is in the hands of the DJs producing it; the whole industry circle hasn't hit yet. There aren't singers, there aren't rappers. Right now it's music for the club." Indeed, the unmixed versions of *tribal* were distant cousins of what we'd just seen in full activation mode. "Same thing happened in reggaeton. Back then, it was simply known as underground." Toy should know: he spent several years signing hip-hop and reggaeton acts for Universal. "In two, three years, there'll be *tribal guarachero* singers and MCs and songs with the rhythm. My head spins thinking that we should be doing it!"

So they did. Toy Selectah formalized his mentor relationship with Rincón, Zavala, and their buddy Alberto Presenda (aka DJ Otto). My article made the rounds. A lighthearted short documentary video that showed rodeo boys from a small town three hours outside Monterrey wearing cowboy boots with ridiculously long points dancing to the music of Erick Rincón went viral. (Toy's prediction came true!) Outside of Mexico, influential DJs began to spike their sets with the sound.

Within months the DJ-production trio now known as 3Ball MTY (tree-BALL Monterrey) rocketed into the Mexican pop stratosphere. Toy Selectah landed them a major-label deal. 3Ball MTY's debut album went gold in Mexico, platinum in the States. The optimistic, club-friendly sound was ubiquitous. The group made regular appearances on TV. 3Ball MTY billboards dotted Los Angeles. When Justin Bieber gave a free concert in the Zócalo for nearly a quarter-million fans, the boys from ArcoIris were the opening act.

I recently caught up with 3Ball MTY at the Hard Rock Cafe in Hollywood. It was one of their many Pepsi promo gigs. Handsome, earnest musicians from humble backgrounds with stable management—what more could advertisers want? Pepsi bankrolled a 3Ball single and accompanying tour. The single shares its title with Pepsi's global slogan for 2013: "Live for Now."

If the organizers had let even a fraction of the enormous

queue of fans outside the Hard Rock franchise onto the dance floor, it could have been a slammin' party. As it was, the room was noticeably underpopulated. Industry suits clumped together on a mezzanine about seventy-five feet from the stage. A crowd toward the front of the dance floor swayed slightly as they held up phones. I suspect it's only a matter of time until this gesture replaces clapping.

Onstage, Rincón, Zavala, and Presenda switched off between drum machines, CD players, and laptops. I appreciated the playful moments of this dynamic, rambunctious performance all the more knowing that many electronic acts of their size rely on a risk-free setup that doesn't allow them to really mix it up the way 3Ball were doing. These kids were respecting the music rather than resting on their laurels in autopilot mode.

The beats morphed into their single "Vive Hoy" (Live for Now). The official video, projected behind them, shows the trio DJing atop a gigantic can of Pepsi as they drink Pepsi from regular-size cans that vanish into wisps of greenish smoke mid-swig, fully compliant with Marx's time-tested maxim that "all that is solid melts into air." High-sugar, fizzy drinks comprise seven out of every ten beverages sold in Mexico, where an estimated one out of six adults suffers from diabetes. Life imitates product-placement videos.

Prophecy and oracles work the same way Pepsi ads do: first the image, then the desire, then, if one is lucky, the goal gets realized. In a semicovert but no less meaningful branding experience, 3Ball MTY's hospitality rider stipulates that twenty-five bottles of PepsiCo water, twenty-five variously branded cans of PepsiCo product, and twenty cans of regular Pepsi be present for each and every performance. If any beverage is gonna appear in the fan pics generated around each performance, it'll be from PepsiCo.

Poorly handled promotional hoopla deserves some ribbing, but don't get me wrong: 3Ball MTY is a success story. As musicians from working-class families in a country without much independent music infrastructure, they've navigated a tricky path. Maybe Ian MacKaye wouldn't approve, but partnering with a major soft-drink brand to reach a wider audience makes a lot of sense. Their art form was populist from its inception. Yet even years after 3Ball's breakthrough, no other *tribal* groups have signed record deals. The industry only supports the trio, treating them as a singularity rather than as artists in an active genre. Who wouldn't want to see neo-Aztec rave music nights in Las Vegas and Berlin? For this to happen 3Ball needs competition, peers.

I ended my early *tribal* essay with "Rincón just gave away 40 tracks of his online, 'for the people who don't have my tunes from 2009 and 2010.' He's naturally generous and knows that the best is yet to come. The stream of kids exiting ArcoIris in time to hop on the free Sunday metro towards home agree—they'll be back next week." Rincón broke the news to me backstage in L.A.: ArcoIris had closed a week after copies of the magazine with my article in it arrived at his family's house.

Club nights shut down (and reopen) all the time. Mostly

they're mediocre and it's no real loss. When the great ones go, an entire artistic ecosystem takes the hit. The culture that birthed 3Ball MTY was as organic as the major-label money elevator that they rose up on was engineered. The ArcoIris DJs were paid about $70 each for a long afternoon of work entertaining thousands. It's excellent that 3Ball made their way outside that low-income hustle, but unless others working within the world of *tribal* get access to similar industry support, the risk is that *tribal guarachero* might cease to be a fertile social space and become a particular sound associated with a single act, whose particularities get rubbed off in the long march through pop.

Imagine if hip-hop were *only* LL Cool J. He links up with Russell Simmons and Rick Rubin to release some landmark singles and commercially successful albums. Mr. Mama Said Knock You Out graduates to become a TV and film personality, hosting the Grammys thirty years later—exactly as happened in real life—except in this scenario there are no other rappers. No Lil Kim, no Eminem, no Kendrick Lamar. A few scattered MCs strive in the underground, but nobody else takes the mantle and turns hip-hop into a proper musical force. It's just a thing that guy who hosts the Grammys did when he was young. If *tribal* doesn't diversify from lauded group to aboveground genre, it could end up in such a situation. Sometimes I wonder if it already has.

3Ball MTY is a test case for what happens when bubbling underground activity reaches up to interact with bright lights and big money. The originators got paid (this is unquestionably good), and even if the scene hasn't yet been able to sustain itself, it might have died off entirely by now if it weren't for 3Ball's mainstream success. But they are there, the main incubator has vanished, and no industry backing has materialized to help creators caught in the fallout.

The sound itself has traveled; it always does. This morning a friend sent me the latest single by one of Nigeria's top rappers, Ice Prince, rhyming over a backing track that was so by-the-book *tribal* that its staccato synths and galloping drums could have been lifted from 3Ball MTY. Ice Prince had tagged the song #Afrobeat, without any mention of *tribal*. No doubt Ice Prince fans will imitate his faithful imitation unaware of its origins. The beat goes on.

NOTHING NEW HERE

Back in Monterrey, Mexico, DJ/producer Javier Estrada has taken the delicious provocations of *tribal* to new heights. He got his start as a heavy-metal drummer. After swapping the drum kit for FruityLoops, he spent some time as a production partner with Erick Rincón before going solo. Javier Estrada has written more than a thousand tracks (using FruityLoops, of course), roughly 430 songs, in the past three years. Estrada's work recognizes that most of the social, geographical, and historical forces that shaped ideas of genre last century cannot be transferred across the narrow bandwidth of cloud-stored musical conversations in the twenty-first century, when clicking a slightly different snare-drum pattern on a screen is sufficient to transform a song from one style to another. In his hands this realization is cause for celebration: all times are available. Genre enters the game as one more formal structure to be played with. The DJ uses a wealth of regional Mexican genres (his beloved pre-Hispanic, *norteño*, *banda*, cumbia, *danzón*, *tribal guarachero*, bolero, mariachi . . .) to frame explorations of international club sounds (house, dubstep, dance rap, and whatever else catches his ear).

Javier Estrada is not against the formal industry, he merely happens to exceed it. Roughly 1 percent of Estrada's songs are available for purchase on some label. The rest can be downloaded, for free, until the ephemeral file-hosting links expire. Further vexing chronology, Estrada maintains no discography. As productive as he is, he does not give us an easy historical-narrative entrée into his oeuvre. The orderly timelines of release schedules and clearly defined back catalogs help make artists legible to us. This is particularly true for music journalism, which still treats the artist album as the primary unit of contemplation and coverage. The superabundance of Estrada's FruityLoops compositions helped me to understand that the program's acolytes promote cyclical time as a worldview: engaging the world not as a start-to-finish symphony but as a proliferation of interlocking, interchangeable loops.

One of DJ culture's most common maxims states that remixing old or ethnic music operates as a bridge connecting folkloric sounds to ecumenical dance floors around the world.

When done correctly, the story goes, reverence and renewal unite in a single gesture that makes the old new. Estrada's music suggests otherwise. His *Norteño Step* EP pits classic *norteño* ballads against dubstep. Estrada wrote *Norteño Step* for his father—inverting the expectation that remixes are for the kids. Instead of viewing the north Mexican regional sounds as something to be updated for global appeal via remix, the EP uses *norteño* as the main attraction, a catalyst for an intergenerational dialogue, and possibly the only way to get his father to come near aggressive dubstep.

Norteño Step's remix of the classic ballad "No Hay Novedad" by Los Cadetes de Linares alternates the original song's bright accordion stabs with gnarly electronic bass riffs—equally loud, equally jarring. Weepy cowboy music and distorted rave sonics tussle without relief or subordination. As is often the case with Estrada, the song name reminds us what's happening: "Nothing New Here." Remixing a famous song about stalled-out time becomes less about refurbishing old sounds for the young and more about putting different temporalities in dialogue.

For everyone who remembers enjoying music in the nineties, that enjoyment came paired with a sense, however foggy, of musical genealogy. Once millions of songs are available at a click and your listening patterns hop around with a whimsy born of erratic search terms and opaque algorithms, timelines explode. Youth of the *tribal* generation access a world of music freed from chronological restraints. The who-did-what-first approach is there if you want it, but "Historical Importance" becomes merely one way of understanding musical proliferation—not progress. The notion of progress itself holds a lot less traction in *tribal* and other branches of loop-based electronic music.

Ahistorical pop could be a grim scenario: people bombarded by the same increasingly similar songs, with the hot new act getting rich by ripping off band X (who ripped off band Y) and playing to fans who know no better, stuck in the Sisyphean Top Forty. To some extent, the scenario is coming true. Spanish researchers analyzed nearly half a million songs from 1955 to 2010 and confirmed that music is becoming more self-similar. Across half a century, they noted more of the same scales, more of the same types of melodies being played on them, and "homogenization of the timbral palette"—even the sonic textures were growing more similiar. The massive reach of an international hit helps to ensure that music, everywhere, slowly bends toward the mainstream. *Tribal guarachero* suggests a way out. These kids are steeped in always-on digital temporality (who isn't?), yet they fuse it with premodern ideas of nonlinearity.

From the start, DJ culture relied on drawing out musical elements from time and space. The DJ mix plays with the tempo of a moving crowd, in large part by pulling sounds from different eras into the same timeline. The *tribal* scene taps into that energy while grounding it with a distinctly Mexican spin by keeping the cyclical, indigenous time of the Aztecs and other original residents of the Americas close at hand. At the most immediate level, it's there in the pre-Colombian musical snippets that work their way across the dance floor, powered by loop-based soft-ware. It also manifests via the temporal mashup artwork: digital pyramids, mixes of graffiti and Aztec drawing styles, and so on.

Tribal guarachero complicates the narratives of newness or progress that propel global dance music. If there is no newness and everything has already happened, then we can jettison related concepts such as "original" or "old" and start listening to music in its promiscuous, iterative glory. Which is how Estrada and countless young musicians make it.

Zooming out, there's an implicit critique of the very idea of progress in *tribal guarachero*. Undocumented workers in America are among the people whose time is literally worth the least. It makes sense that a Mexican working-class music has built up an enormously strong youth culture based on engaging with past times and loop-based, low-authorship music.

In the hands of Estrada and the *tribaleros*, Elias Canetti's claim that "a civilization comes to an end when a people no longer takes its own chronology seriously" becomes a kind of rallying cry. *Tribal*'s vibrations shake and shiver with the hope that certain wrongs can be righted, tempered by the knowledge that history in reverse will merely flip the bad guys around.

9

HOW TO HOLD ON?

Give me the flute and sing
For singing is the secret to eternity
And the sound of the flute remains
After the end of existence.
   —FAIRUZ, "Aatini al Nay wa Ghanni"

It all comes back. It all comes back. It all
   comes back. It all comes back.
Is this my beginning?
   —D'CRUZE, "Come Back"

The work of Javier Estrada and other musicians who make their material available for free download presents a simple problem: How do you catalog that much sound? A few years back visionary British rapper/producer Wiley tweeted out links to eleven ZIP files containing more than eighty songs—including some from his major-label record deal, which the free giveaway derailed. Some dedicated followers made their own "best of" compilations out of it. Many, like me, dipped in and were overwhelmed. Messy files and digital superabundance can flummox even the most ardent fan. It seems possible—barely—to keep everything.

Or impossible not to try. Let whoever cares distinguish between the durable and the disposable. *Right-click* what you love, *save as*.

With physical stuff, preservation means helping the object remain itself. Hundred-year-old shellac records can still deliver the soul and swing of the musicians captured therein. Preservation of digital "objects" asks of us the opposite: make multiples from this unique piece of data and ensure that they are fluid enough to be shepherded from one storage format to another. To hang on to digital info, one needs whatever physical carrier contains the zeros and ones of the file (even an MP3 occupies physical space), as well as the necessary software or operating system required to play back that data. Proprietary hardware; content whose use, storage, and movement is restricted by digital rights management (DRM) techniques; and fly-by-night file-sharing sites all make it very hard for today's librarians to do their work. How old is the oldest MP3 in your collection?

To save. It's a slippery verb. In digital domains, to save means to destroy information and replace the data with altered information bearing the same name. The only time one needs to save a digital file is when it has changed, and the only way to save a file in the sense of *to rescue* or *to keep* is to copy it, which replicates it in a new place, sacrificing any uniqueness in favor of ubiquity.

Of course, for millennia sound couldn't be recorded or kept. The best one could do was jot down the notes and attempt to indicate how they were to be played. The unique flavor of an instrument, a singer, a band joined in song? These were things you experienced in the moment or not at all. Then Thomas Edison came along and showed us how to write sound waves down. His 1877 invention was as much a metaphysical innovation as a mechanical one. Suddenly music could travel without musicians. Voices left their bodies and began to outlive their speakers. Performance spun into playback. Pandora's jukebox opened up.

By the early 1900s the technology had developed from bulky cylinders of tin and wax into the basic format we know today: a thin disc with sound waves cut into the grooves on each side. Those early discs are called 78s, after the rpm speed they spun at, or shellacs, for the material they were made of: two parts stone for every one part lacquer. Shellacs dominated the market until vinyl gained a foothold in the 1950s. Vinyl cost more but broke less. More than half a century later, vinyl remains a stellar format for audio storage. A quick look at the rarest records in the universe helps explain why.

The LP's consumer heyday peaked in 1977 with the all-time high of 344 million albums sold in the States alone. That year, weed-smoking celebrity astrophysicist Carl Sagan teamed up with NASA to shoot a pair of golden records deep into interstellar space. Spacecraft *Voyager 1* and *2* are currently exiting our solar system at a zippy thirty-five thousand miles per hour. On the outside of each vehicle a golden disc sleeved in a protective metal casing nestles among the astronomical probes. The record comes equipped with a custom cartridge and needle and playback-speed instructions explaining rpm in terms of atomic constants. No turntable is included; humanity's first far-reaching message to aliens is "Wanna hear what we have to say? Build a turntable, buddy."

Mixtape as love letter from Gaia to all the aliens out there.

Audio was selected to showcase the diversity of life on earth. The *Voyager* LPs contain whale song and Chuck Berry, Bach and dogs barking, and humans sending greetings in so many languages that intelligent extraterrestrials might mistake this Babel mantra for a complex music that prizes nonrepetition. Ann Druyan, the project's creative director, and Carl Sagan fell in love as they worked on the Golden Record; a recording of her brain waves translated into sound and touted as "the brainwaves of a young woman in love" are on there too.

The *Voyager* LPs were more than a mere PR stunt. That vinyl records' intergenerational cool resulted from an elegant fusion of physics and poetics was not lost on NASA's team. Canny science popularizer Sagan used the Golden Record to celebrate thinking on a civilizational scale. How to preserve something for millions of years? What might we humans want to tell long-distance aliens about ourselves? And what might a common ground on which to base interspecies interplanetary communication look like, anyway?

Any alien clever enough to notice the spacecraft whistling through our unimaginably empty universe should be sharp enough to figure out that the golden LP grooves translate into a scaled-up portrait of the wave activity we understand as sound. Under a microscope a record reveals grooves that are directly *analogous* to audio waves. In contrast, any digitally encoded audio would be nothing more than a gibberish smear of zeros and ones to the extraterrestrials. Digital domains require levels of abstraction; analog recording systems have a direct relationship with what they represent.

Even if the aliens' physiognomy doesn't contain anything earlike, they should be able to work out that this spectrum of vibrational energy was important to us crudely technologized apes. Maybe Steve Martin's *Saturday Night Live* skit was right— the aliens will contact us with a single, urgent request: "Send more Chuck Berry!"

Another reason why phonographs are a good choice for intergalactic messaging: they're robust. A gold-coated copper record is tough enough to weather the extreme temperature, radiation, and magnetic fields of outer space, conditions that would fry all other formats. "Shelf life of a billion years," boasted Sagan, lead selector behind the most well-traveled mixtape of all. When the fuel runs out and the batteries go cold, these gilded records will still ferry along a strangely hopeful message to the stars—that some entities might find them and glimpse how our planet sounded way back in 1977.

Although the one-two punch of cassettes followed by compact discs ultimately knocked vinyl out at the end of the twentieth century, LPs can still fire up our collective imagination the way that eight-tracks, CDs, minidiscs, tapes, hard drives, and USB trinkets can't. Even before its recent upswing as a boutique product, vinyl held on to popularity longer than any other recorded music format and remains more durable than the competition. Indeed, practically the only music I created during the nineties that can still be heard are a few songs I pressed on vinyl. The CD-R masters, the digital audiotape recordings, and the old hard drives conked out years ago.

BEIRUT

How to hold on?

The question was raised everywhere I turned during a recent trip to Beirut, and I was lucky enough to spend time with musicians who've dedicated their lives to answering it.

Lebanon's capital city has been continuously inhabited for at least five thousand years. I knew little about the small, complicated place before arriving to DJ and give a talk about *Sufi Plug Ins*—invited, indirectly, by some Serbians. After dropping off my bags, my host whisked me away to a café. Outside, the first thing I noticed was the smell. I'd never been in a city that smelled quite this good. Certain streets smelled of jasmine, lilac, juniper, orange blossom. By surviving, blooming, these plants speak to another order inhabiting the city, one rooted in seasonal time. Everything felt Euro-chic until my host pointed out the bullet-strafed facade of the apartment block in front of us. We saw plenty of these—the damaged and occasionally half-destroyed buildings serving as memorials to the recent civil war, flanked by multinational clothing chains and telecom outlets.

Saudi-financed construction sites literally steamroll downtown Beirut's history into a hypercommercial present, based on a kitsch interpretation of the past. Soulless as they seem, the slick Saudi shopping centers arrive prehaunted with the threat of future blowouts, which are so present in this city. Yet it's not uncommon to orient oneself by architectural ghosts. For decades after it was bombed into oblivion, the Beydoun Mosque still served as a reference point. Sometimes you can tell a taxi driver the name of a prominent shopping mall or movie theater, say, and he'll have no idea what you are talking about: his internal map charts a city no longer there. Globalization is the story of how ghosts die.

A hijabied Gulf Arab walked by me radiating glamour in high heels and Louis Vuitton handbag, her face taped up from a recent nose job. The construction worker in paint-stained jeans who strolled past a half block later safeguarded his new nose under fresh bandages too. When social media demand that people constantly produce positive images of themselves, covering up isn't a possibility: plastic surgery becomes a new veil. When I picture a future without wonky noses or creaky old buildings that bear traces of their past lives, I get sad. The drive to standardize leaps from bone structure to infrastructure without stopping.

Architecture—real or imagined—prompts memory so efficiently because our brains are hardwired to recall things-in-places and unusual or disturbing scenes. Memory-quiz champions envision fantastic images that correspond to what they want to remember and "place" each icon in some specific nook of their mental building. These mnemonic aids are called memory palaces. Their effectiveness speaks to how when a place is destroyed or erased, all the personal histories linked to it slip further into the past.

Clara Sfeir, the woman who presented at the conference immediately before me, did not speak—she danced, to the sound of an old 78 shellac recording that was so crackly it seemed like Japanese noise at times. After my talk, she invited me to meet her husband, Mustafa Said, a musician who directs the Arab Music Archiving and Research Foundation (AMAR). Late nineteenth-century and early twentieth-century Middle Eastern recordings form the bulk of AMAR's collection, one of the largest of its kind. The foundation's work centers around how to preserve their collection and present it to the public. This means everything from digitizing their shellac collection to producing an exhaustively researched podcast with English-language transcriptions. Their website is a growing repository of information, accompanied by CDs, monographs, and the occasional public talk or concert. They have been known to track down fans who recorded radio concerts on tape in the 1940s— it's all part of piecing together a half-lost history. AMAR believes in an ongoing conversation with the past in this city busy erasing most traces of it.

Taxiing en route to AMAR past the French airs of the corniche, I could have been in Miami or any other ocean-hugging city contoured by high-volume transnational cash flows. English-language signage advertised laser hair removal at competitive rates. Brazilians in the Middle East! We cruised past a Hardee's. Pope Benedict XVI presided over the mix, smiling down from enormous Arabic-language billboards that announced his recent visit: "I give you my peace."

The cityscape cross-faded into the port's industrial waterfront, and from there our taxi switchbacked up into the hills. Traffic thinned as we rose, the city's heat receding. Dramatic curves offered glimpses of Beirut, alternately smudged and glittering through the midday haze. Who knew that in exactly a week this view's idyll would be interrupted by columns of smoke: Lebanon's top security official, Wissam al-Hassan, killed by a car bomb. Such violence drives sales of the Ma2too3a smartphone app, which sends out real-time updates with the locations of protest tire burnings and other civil unrest. It debuted at the top of Beirut's iTunes store charts.

My cabbie's name was Tame. His close-cropped, gel-spiked hair and Adidas tracksuit reminded me that soccer fashion is another great globalizer. Tame was pumping the latest *dabke* through the car's overworked speakers. The style is popular all over the Levant, and in places where the diaspora gathers, such as Brooklyn's Bay Ridge. This Lebanese variant involved men stamping and chant-singing in unison over thumping electronic beats. I asked where to buy it. Better than shopping tips, Tame invited me to grab some off his phone via Bluetooth. He insisted that I take last year's big hit, which runs for more than half an hour. Even if you don't enjoy *dabke*, it's impossible to be mad at any pop tradition where songs clock in at such extravagant lengths. I cracked open my laptop, located his device, *IMPOŞIB£€ £OV€*, and started the transfer.

Casual exchanges with strangers form an important part of what it means to live in a city, and I love that Bluetooth encourages that slim social bond. For an exchange to work, the giver and the receiver must be within a few yards of each other. Bluetooth's human sense of scale is marvelous. Its wireless protocol requires closeness—usually a face-to-face conversation—not distance.

As the transfer completed, I noticed that my American

laptop, unable to grasp the incoming Arabic file names, had labeled Tame's MP3s in a clatter of random characters. Educated young Beirutis effortlessly switch between accent-free English and Arabic. Everyday computer technology collapses when trying to do the same. The artists' names and song titles get lost in translation, meaning that this particular batch of sonic goodness just became a lot harder to identify.

Tame pulled to the curb in front of a medieval church. A short walk from the church brought us to a villa looking out over the hills toward the Mediterranean beyond. The owner, a well-to-do music fan, underwrites AMAR, which is situated at the end of a winding stone path through his orchard. The vista was a rare treat. Less obvious but no less valuable was the quiet, whose nuances communicated the sensation of unobstructed space between here and the sea. The hillside's expanse muted what few sounds there were.

Calming acoustics continue inside AMAR's Spartan yet welcoming space, which enjoys a high ceiling and a Swiss sense of order. Four people were at work, though the airy room could accommodate many more. Near the entrance, one woman played oud for another in a corner nook formed by sound-buffer walls. They were recording episodes for AMAR's podcast series, one of the organization's first forays into sharing its work with the greater public.

The building's easygoing openness reinforces the sense that work here happens on a tangible level. It's Bluetoothy. The archive lies within reach, literally: sliding shelves house AMAR's collection of around seven thousand shellacs and six thousand hours of tape recordings. Vintage gramophones plugged into high-end computers translate these rare pieces of an analog past into digital formats.

At this scale an individual's effort can mean the archive's success or failure, a far cry from the museum-as-warehouse-of-culture approach or the distant digital lockers of some privately controlled "cloud." Against those impersonal catchall containers, I prefer to call AMAR's archive a *memory palace*.

AMAR director Mustafa Said is a caustic and original thinker, a contrarian preservationist unconcerned with conforming to anyone's expectations. He's blind, but doesn't wear dark glasses to hide the way his eyes twitch and roll. Said's not in the business of making anyone comfortable with trivialities. That would be a pretense.

He sat at a desk in the middle of AMAR, typing away at a stubby laptop. The machine was equipped with text-to-speech software so Said could hear what he typed and navigate through the PC's menus. His fingers blurred across the keyboard, sending the stilted robot voice machine-reading at speeds so fast it sounded like a computer's muttering subconscious: *space bar eye tea question mark space bar shift . . .* This spill of clipped syllables is Said's primary interface with the digital. We can do countless previously unimaginable things with vocal processing these days—from Auto-Tune hyperreality to the glottal yells of monsters in the latest blockbuster. But this text-to-speech software remains painful to hear. It depicts the digital world with a blunt honesty, without distractions by pretty graphic interfaces or pleasant voices based on human speech samples. The zero/one binary logic of the digital marks an alien presence. Interpretation, gradation, paradox, intuition—we are resolutely analog beings steeped in these things. Hearing this chemical voice reminded me, quite coldly, of that nonhuman thing at the core of the computer touching me at every screen.

Said finished typing, the computer stopped speaking, and we folded ourselves into chairs to chat about how he got started.

Mustafa Said discussed entropy. Political upheaval sent his grandparents from financial comfort to penny-pinching. Thieves scattered his grandfather's records on the floor—worthless weight!—to take the bookshelves that held them. Having witnessed the money slide, he sidestepped into another type of value. Said's grandmother presented him with books on philosophy and art, and these were what took hold. A handful of salvaged records from his grandfather seeded Said's collection. "I don't give a shit about my family history!" said Said, quick to reject any easy relationship between his music preservation and his family's record of loss. That's noise, a common story, humanity's background hiss. He's here for the music.

When Said was eleven, he secretly learned the twenty-minute walk to school through Cairo's chaotic streets in order to pocket his bus money. After a year and a half of unaccompanied walks, he'd saved enough to buy a toylike oud with plastic strings.

Said got in trouble with the Egyptian authorities for participating in political protests, and I suspect that if he hadn't left his country in his early twenties to study music across the Arab world, he might be incarcerated now, for he's one of those combative, conscientious individuals who believes in a better world strong enough to decry the stupidities of the one we inhabit in the presence of those with power. In all our conversations he swears with gusto across a variety of languages. The preservationist lets it be known that he's not a prude.

These days, Said's fight lies in advocating *IMPOSIBЄЄ £OVЄ* for the worlds that left their traces as written sounds. Said sees AMAR's work of preserving these shellacs as part of a wider effort to recuperate Arab history. AMAR archives a group of key artists whose relevance to Middle Eastern musical history is comparable, in Said's consideration, to a Bach or Wagner in the West.

The wave of European-led modernization that changed the course of Arabic music brought with it the very gear that made recording and distributing that music possible in the first place.

At the microscale: musicians huddled around a gramophone horn, playing their hearts out as the contraption (likely as not in the early years leased from the British Gramophone Company) froze their music onto a lacquer plate. The gramophone's ear dictated the layout of bodies in the room: the loudest instruments were positioned farthest from the horn so as not to overwhelm the recording. The main vocalist had pride of place.

Said eased a shellac from 1905 onto a gramophone and turned the hand crank. Yusuf Al-Manyalawi's voice sprang to life. The sound waves that bounced down into the lacquer a century ago free themselves as the needle digs in again. AMAR's collection offers a slow-motion portrait of those critical moments of tradition in transition, carried on the few shellacs that have reached us unbroken.

"Serene and bashful, [Al-Manyalawi] executed melodies with precision, leaving no room for redundancy," writes Said. "He preferred expressing his emotions in the classical poems by raising his voice at discreet and subtle points." Said's write-up is a kind of poetry in itself: he's able to extract a depth of information from these 78s that few others can. Manyalawi's talent was such that his record sales dominated the market for two decades after his 1911 death, yet now he requires translation of sorts, bridges such as Said who can tell us where and how to listen. The past is an overgrown garden.

At AMAR they debate whether to archive the sound that comes out of the gramophone horn, to capture its unique acoustics, or to take the signal directly from the needle, the way modern turntables do. As the elders heard it or as the machine understands it? How best to coax this ghost into the present?

Behind the technical questions lies a larger one. What is worth saving? AMAR aims its preservation efforts at the dawn of recording, yet we've seen how culture created in all-digital ecosystems is equally if not more fragile.

I decided to troll Said a little bit. "What about Haifa Wehbe?" Lebanese pop star Haifa looks like a member of the Kardashian clan. With her relentlessly commercial songs, surgically augmented sex appeal, and casual racism, Wehbe represents the

Lebanese music mainstream at its most horrifyingly efficient. Aesthetes find her repellent.

"Mustafa, doesn't Haifa's work deserve to be preserved? She needs to be included in the picture if folks look back on these years." The lowest-common-denominator "background music" of any epoch is almost always eye-opening, although I admit it can quickly turn into empty-calorie pap.

"We've already done that!" he snapped, then started naming artists who sang bawdy songs a century before Haifa. She's old news to Said.

The money behind high culture and the sheer proliferation of popular culture provide each with much of its staying power: museums and foundations such as AMAR for the former; piracy sites and YouTube flotsam for the latter. All too big to be easily forgotten. What about the fleeting hits of corniche teen culture, folk song, all the styles bubbling up on the edges?

AMAR strikes me as one of the finest possible responses to the 1932 Cairo Congress. Not only does it continue their mission of Arab music preservation and education, but the same sounds that were being fretted over back then are of primary interest to Said and crew. I first found out about the Congress when I came across a few of the recording sessions issued on CD, and I suspect that AMAR's bilingual Web archive may serve as a similar magnet. The ideological debates about what music is worthy of study feel echoed as well. AMAR's archive complicates and enriches the histories of early modern Arab music, yet, like all archives, it simultaneously buries other histories by keeping them on the outside.

AMAR makes me think that any archive worth its salt needs to reflect the quirks of the individuals tasked to maintain it. The art historical canon looks back on the past not with twenty-twenty hindsight but rather with a kind of fuzzy near-blindness—only the biggest figures stand out. This modest Beirut archive reminds me of how fleeting greatness can be, and how handmade; idiosyncratic histories of music are the only ones that we can hold close the way we do songs.

Don't take my word for it. Even if you have no taste for scratchy old shellacs, you can enjoy Said's archly brilliant online write-ups of these forgotten giants. Discussing Abd al-Hay Hilmî, "the spoiled child of Egyptian high society at the turn of the century," Said writes:

> Hilmî would leave a concert he was hired for if he failed to notice a pleasant-looking face, be it male or female, in the audience, and preferred to sing for handsome strangers ... He ended up worn by his excesses, which caused him an angina pectoris, and died whilst drunken in Alexandria after a feast of sea turtle ... A self-taught artist in learned tradition, Abd al-Hay Hilmî insisted on ignoring the rules. His well-known lack of respect for rhythm and composition made him an easy target for harsh criticism from rigorists who were subjugated by Western patterns with their sanctification of the composer's role. His passion naturally finds its best expression in *mawawil*, where nonmetrical improvisation is the only rule. In this field, he remains unmatchable.

IMPROVISATION

A few days after visiting AMAR, I go to see Said at his downtown apartment. Director Mustafa Said's preservation efforts are complemented by his interest in performance and improvisation. (The polymath rigorist writes music too, though he's not "subjugated by Western patterns with their sanctification of the composer's role.") As our talk of music drifted to other matters, Said's houseguest Mahmoud Turkmani picked up his guitar. Inside I shouted for joy. On the surface, I had another pastry and sipped my tea. I'd missed his and Said's public performance earlier in the month and had been hoping that I'd get to hear them play here in Said's living room, but that's not the sort of thing you can up and ask for.

Turkmani's first notes appeared random. He was articulating the scale and establishing a cadence. Not a song but the shape of a song's becoming. Behind the couches twelve ouds were tumbled in a pile like discarded toys, which was surprising because the rest of the house was so orderly. Said's newest oud lay on a table near him. Lately he has been giving a master builder intricate directions on how to make his custom ouds sound even better, and this one was the finest to date. As Turkmani's notes acquired direction, Said reached for the oud, then set its twelve strings asparkle with staccato bursts zigzagging against Turkmani's steady field. A pattern began to form—I grasped it several beats after the musicians, and now that repetition had made the musical structure clear, it could and did change.

The seeming effortlessness with which lifelong musicians summon voices from their instruments always takes my breath away. A guitar, in my hands, is just a strangely shaped piece of wood, a book in a language I can't read. I whipped out my phone to grab some video, then my thumb froze above the touch screen. If I recorded it, I'd never watch it. These unrepeatable moments are as throwaway as they are priceless—they have to be. There's value in being as free and as lost as all the music before Edison. Improvisation gives lightness to history's weight.

Maya Angelou claimed she knew why the caged bird sings in her famous poem: "For the caged bird / sings of freedom." I think she was wrong. It's not about freedom. It's about abundance, the compulsion to create instants when the song takes over. We'll throw this beauty away since we can always make more. This moment is the heart of the matter. A true song is not *about* freedom; it enacts freedom by creating a body with its own rules and giving you enough clues to reach its heart on its own terms. The best songs give form to impossible love. They shape it, and us, from a place outside time, where their own best conditions are realized. Listening, we go there. Then the moment ends.

Said and Turkmani stopped abruptly, shrugged, and laughed.

I think about what stories get told when Mustafa plays his oud, and who, if anyone, can store that information.

I think about what's escaping in every library and music

shop destroyed over the Syrian border forty miles away. History spiraled into 78s offers a surprisingly resilient alternative to the twitchy, glitchy tinderbox of modern living.

I begin to understand why Said fights for his tinny shellacs. Those terabytes of rescued songs at AMAR form Mustafa Said's lengthening shadow, thrown into relief when his figure hits the light. In Beirut, as elsewhere, to set down roots may be a far more radical strategy than to try to shape the future. If we can hear the ways in which what was lovely and as light as spring a hundred years ago remains lovely today, then maybe we can frame things for an uncertain future. Not beauty but the conditions for beauty's becoming. Improvisation calls on a spirit of interdependence and can only happen when you are free to move in any direction.

Recorded sound vibrates between history and pleasure. Live sound exists only in the present. It cannot linger. This is one of the reasons why sound defines public space even more than architecture. Kids jamming that week's hit, neighbors fucking behind a thin wall, the call to prayer's divine layer competing with traffic's blare, the loud low boom of something blowing up—and its opposite, hilltop garden quiet.

To remember the world is to remember the sound of the world. To listen carelessly is to forget. Our lives spool down to whatever medium can recall us: wet brains, hard drives, magnetic tapes, circular pieces of plastic inscribed with tiny mountains of sound that came from bodies and moved bodies, somewhere, just in time, then running out of it.

REFUGEE LIBRARY

After the rarefied heights of AMAR's archival efforts, a chance connection with a song gave me entrée to see what's happening at the other end of the spectrum, where some of the city's poorest and least powerful residents deal with music and memory.

I first encountered "Sabra et Chatila" by Moroccan group Nass El Ghiwane on a cassette. It was love at first listen. "Sabra et Chatila" opens with a long banjo melody. A single-note guembri bass line thrums alongside the banjo, paced at about four pulses a second, steadying in its rhythm yet unsettling in its speed. Vocals enter angled between statement and lament. The changeover that happens after a few minutes reboots the song's entire perspective. The guembri steps to the forefront with a simplified lead melody as the banjo eases into support mode. The leader and the follower have exchanged positions. There's no room for hierarchy maintenance in a groove such as this. Two percussionists enter and intensify the piece.

Whether the Moroccan rhythmic sensibility's combination of subtlety and drive is the result of evolution in a geographic sweet spot or some other enormous gift, "Sabra et Chatila" showcases one of its main lessons to me: the notion that responsibility, understood as rhythm, is shared among all players present. As the song winds down, language leaves the singing but the emotion stays, transformed into plaintive humming. Closed lips don't stop the voices from sounding.

The arc of "Sabra et Chatila," from lonely beginning to full group, renders a sense of life's tragic side tempered by resilience, comforted by the company of others. Years later I learned that the lyrics memorialize one of the Arab world's most notorious massacres. The Shatila Palestinian refugee camp is shored against the Sabra neighborhood in southeast Beirut. In 1982, Israeli army forces cordoned off the area and allowed a right-wing Lebanese militia to enter on a three-day spree of murder and rape that left thousands of civilians dead—mostly Palestinian, mostly women, children, and old men.

A grim history and a breathtaking song. When a friend going there to meet with a Palestinian human rights worker invited me to come along, I leaped at a chance to visit.

When we met at her apartment a short bus ride from Shatila, I was instantly at ease: Samira, a sassy fiftysomething full of laughter and generosity, could pass for one of my aunts. She fed us lunch as we made plans to regroup for a Shatila visit in the following days, when she could make sure her people were there. I was after music, and she knew everyone.

The next day we headed over. Established in 1949 as a temporary refuge for Palestinians fleeing war and expulsion in what had just become Israel, Shatila now also houses poor Lebanese, Syrians, East Africans, and many others with limited means and bad passports. But its heartbeat remains Palestinian. A dirt field lay at the camp's entrance. No children played there. A crumpled red banner at the back read SHATILA MASSACRE.

After that stillness the rest of Shatila bustled with hawkers and storefronts and a river of people that we navigated for ten minutes. Samira greeted friends right and left. Before we arrived, Samira had requested that if anyone asked, I was to say that I was from South Africa instead of America. We didn't want problems with the wrong people.

So much of life happens in public in neighborhoods as crowded as Shatila. A sense of community descends whether or not it is sought, defined in large part by the lack of aural privacy. Whenever you play music, you can be sure someone else hears it.

At last we dipped into a music shop. Or a distributor. Or a bootlegging operation. Likely all three. A quick look at the colorful CDs stacked on the floor and I was excited to start—no, there was no stopping here. Samira waved to the proprietor as she led us through the rear storeroom and out some sudden door. The streets narrowed across a few more turns until we ended up in an alleyway plastered by Che Guevara graffiti. Tibetan prayer flags adorned a tangle of electricity cables overhead. The cables intertwined with laundry lines as the floors rose. An elderly man on a plastic lawn chair cradled an AK-47 in his lap. I pictured him there every day, fading imperceptibly from month to month like the prayer flags that trembled above his head. Palestinians cannot hold white-collar jobs or own property in Lebanon. So they work odd jobs. They make do. They wait.

Our destination was a no-name shop on the alley's bend. Inside, a man sat at a desk sagging under the weight of a desktop computer. His cigarette smoke swirled into miniature storm clouds above his head. Flag key chains, kitschy wood carvings, and other Palestine trinkets coated the walls. No music in sight.

After the flag the most common image in the shop was Palestinian cartoonist Naji al-Ali's iconic Handala character. This
simple line drawing of a young, barefoot child in ragged clothes
with its back to the viewer has come to symbolize Palestinian
self-determination. The figure repeated across a variety of merchandise. "Even though he is rough, he smells of amber," wrote
al-Ali, who lived in a tent in Shatila for several years.

Refugee time is implacable. Bureaucratic machinery and in-
difference propel it erratically, if at all. To better grasp what it's
like to be subjected to that type of time, I think about Kraftwerk, the pioneering techno-pop band from Germany. Theirs is
a music of the autobahn, reveling in unchecked travel and the
comforts of regular control. It could only have been made by a
culture confident in the power of its passport. Sounds reflecting
a world free of roadblocks, slicked by cheap energy. Their most
well-known song, "Trans-Europe Express," is a fantasia of unre-
stricted movement. Others, such as "Europe Endless" and "Autobahn," anthemize the highway network connecting Europe, as
friction-free as their shimmering synthesizer lines or weightlessly
funky drum-machine parts. Releasing albums with lyrics in
English, French, and German completes Kraftwerk's embrace
of a transparent, all-things-equal world.

"Driving is fun," said Kraftwerk's percussionist Wolfgang Flür
"We had no speed limit on the autobahn, we could race through
the highways, through the Alps . . . We used to drive a lot, we used
to listen to the sound of driving, the wind, passing cars and lor-
ries, the rain, every moment the sounds around you are changing, and the idea was to rebuild those sounds on the synth."

Waiting is not fun. Is it possible to make music sprung from the condition of waiting, styles that voice what that situation feels like as surely as Kraftwerk used their foundational hypnotic motorik to evoke the no-speed-limit highway system? Music born from the Handala drawing, with its face turned away from us, perhaps.

Samira explained that I was a musician interested in hearing some quality Palestinian songs. This led to an animated discussion among Samira, the owner, and their friends who drifted into the store and stayed because of the spectacle triggered by my presence. *Play him that. No, no, no, forget him, he's a terrible singer, he needs to hear this. But did you consider this? You think that's good Palestinian music? You must be crazy . . .* Periodically the shopkeeper blasted a song, whereupon everyone looked at me for signs of approval. I nodded yea or nay—*Well, no surprise he's not into that lousy singer, give him some of this instead . . .* The owner kept mumbling, "He wants so-and-so," generally wrong about what I was looking for. This is how you end up with the Palestinian Hit Parade in your music collection. Nationalist pop songs at headache-inducing volume combined with off-brand-cigarette smoke had me feeling faint. A roomful of people unpretentiously trying to sound out a bit of national concord as they interpret or anticipate the desires of a stranger who can't quite express them. I could barely breathe. Was this what true democracy felt like?

As the owner scrolled through folders on his enormous old-school computer, I thought of him less like a shopkeeper and more like a librarian. The pieces of culture here had not been

collected to be sold. In fact, it seemed downright silly to consider this jumble some kind of music store. A very different sensibility organized the music we were sifting through. A desktop
PC straining in the heat, half-malware, half–folder soup: this
is a library of Palestinian music today. A handful of guys like
this in every camp. It's preservation through propagation,
and if low-resolution sound files are what's spreading it around,
so be it.

Then the guy beside me asked where I was from. "I guess
you could say . . ." I trailed off into silence. South Africa? I know
nothing about the place. *Apartheid*, I thought. What else? Paul
Simon and Ladysmith Black Mambazo and those people Sha-
rifa hung out with in Cape Town. What if he'd visited or lived
there and asked me a follow-up question? In my line of work I
constantly run into Africans and Arabs in unlikely cities who,
upon discovering that I'm an American, pull out staff ID cards
from when they worked at the Magic Kingdom in Orlando.
The ones who didn't work for Disney unfold a worn photo of
themselves posing with someone who looks like Dionne War-
wick. *She's my friend, see!* I want to believe.

American pop mythology radiates the world. But so do our
weapons, our foreign-policy maneuvers. At that moment I was
a quintessential U.S. citizen: ignorant of geography, buffered by
passport privilege, dangerously naive about world history, a
smiling man-child with teeth straightened by braces, nosing
about more or less uninvited, about to lie to incredibly nice
hosts.

"Uhhh, I mean"—the more I tried to modulate disbelief

out of my voice, the more American it sounded. Samira grinned a lovely conspiratorial grin and raised her eyebrows. With strained confidence I squeaked out, "I'm from South Africa." Time hung like a slow Web connection. Then the guy pressed a hand on my shoulder and said, "We love Nelson Mandela." Samira clasped her hands together, giggling. National identity as tragicomedy.

My selections continued. Once in a while the owner stopped to burn me a CD-R. I'd asked for data CD-Rs so that my computer could (I hoped) see the artist names and song titles. This didn't happen, for reasons I never fully understood. Instead I got MP3s burned as audio files (transcoding in full effect), which effectively wiped them of all identifying metadata. Future listeners may have access to everything ever recorded—with no reliable indication of what it is or when it was made. No way of following that thread back to the past and the musicians who voiced it.

We walked out of the shop into rain. People sheltered under awnings. The vegetable stands looked splendid, produce fresh and glistening. Samira hopped over the rapidly forming puddles in two-inch clog heels. I followed in her footsteps. "American, hello!" called someone. As a seasoned South African traveler, I knew better than to respond, and besides, he was selling socks.

Samira pressed a bundle of cinnamon bark into my hand as a parting gift. We are trapped in our skins; what understanding does not begin with the body? And if national laws shape various bodies into a people, then food and music give the people their bodies back: eat, listen, sway, dance to this.

OINK

I wouldn't have thought of that smoky room in Shatila as the future of the library if I hadn't known Oink.

Music and software file-sharing site Oink changed the way I thought about the music industry and digital commons. I'd heard rumors of Oink for years but hadn't seen the members-only site until I was invited to join by a friend in early 2007. Oink was anal, Oink was comprehensive. The site administrators were fierce about quality—only clean rips from CD or vinyl releases could be posted. Many releases were even posted as audiophile-quality FLAC files. (Shockingly, even now the big digital music sites such as iTunes and Amazon still don't give you the option to purchase CD-quality digital files.) Uploading an incomplete album or neglecting to provide detailed tracklist information could get you kicked off. No unofficial collections or concert recordings were permitted.

In many cases, downloading an album from Oink was faster (more on this in a bit) *and* gave you more information about the music than commercial sites. Think about that . . . a free website providing speedy downloads of music at equivalent or higher quality than the paid music sites. And it had an incredibly deep collection of both new and old releases, usually in a variety of file formats and bitrates. It was overwhelming! My first thought was *Wow, Oink is an amazing library.* Second thought: *Wow, I really need to start selling DJ Rupture T-shirts. Album sales will only continue to drop, and I gotta make money somehow!*

My library metaphor for Oink makes more sense than economic analogies: for digital music and data, there's lots of demand *but no scarcity at all*, which either requires that we rebuild an economic model not based on supply and demand or start embracing commons analogies. I like living from my music, but I also like libraries, the ideas behind libraries.

Oink had *everything* by certain artists. Literally everything. I searched for "DJ Rupture" and found every release I'd ever done, from an obscure 7-inch on a Swedish label to 320 Kbps rips of my first 12-inch, self-released back in 1999. It was shocking. And reassuring. Out there in the Web, shared across hundreds of users' hard drives, lay my entire catalog. I myself didn't have all my own music in one place. Oink did, and I loved it for that. The big labels want music to equal money, but as much as anything else, music is memory, as priceless and worthless as memory.

About a week after I shipped out orders of the first live CD-R that the Ex guitarist Andy Moor and I released, it appeared on Oink. Someone who had purchased it directly from me turned around and torrented it on Oink. I wasn't mad, I was just more stunned by the reach and usefulness of the site.

If sharing copyrighted music without paying for it were legal, then Oink was the best music website in the world. For fans, consideration of the music comes before questions of money and ownership—this is how it should be. Any system that doesn't take that into account as a central fact is going to generate a lot of friction. When I say *system*, I mean everything from Sony to iTunes to white-label 12-inches that cost £8 in

London shops and only have two songs on them. (I was mail-ordering a lot of these to Barcelona in 2006. It hurt.)

Oink didn't offer solutions; it highlighted the problems of overpriced, overcontrolled music elsewhere. Oink was an online paradise for music fans. The only people who could truly be mad at it were the ones directly profiting from the sale of digital or physical music—such as myself.

Like many BitTorrent sites, Oink enforced what's called share ratios. In a nutshell, share ratios mean that each user must upload a certain amount of data in relation to what they download. This feature encourages generosity and rewards people who keep making music available to others. Oink's minimum share ratio was 0.20, meaning that if you downloaded five albums, you then had to upload around one album's worth of music, data equaling one-fifth the amount you nabbed from Oink users. If you only took and never gave, or if you shared, but not enough, then you'd eventually get kicked off.

Watching Oink work helped me to understand the structural intelligence of BitTorrent architecture. The information being splashed around is stored in users' computers. Peer to peer. With BitTorrent, most folks downloading the same files also upload the bits they grab, so everybody gets fast download speeds. If there's a rush to download popular files hosted on one server, people will experience incredibly slow speeds, or even server crash. Whereas with BitTorrent's genius architecture, the more popular any specific file is, the faster everyone's speeds will be, since there'll be many peers with copies of the same file. Post-scarcity: the network becomes stronger as participation goes up. Thus a popular album (or a legal copy of the Linux operating system) can be grabbed in minutes with a decent Internet connection.

Oink, like BitTorrent itself, became stronger and faster the more people used it—scalability writ large. Folks wanted to share, to maintain high share ratios. New releases were highly valued. But Oinkers kept older releases available as well (you never know when someone will want your Norwegian proto-death-metal collection, so you keep your bandwidth open). Whether you call it distributed *tape-sharing* (to use an eighties term) or distributed *piracy* (to use a nineties industry term), Oink, using BitTorrent and meticulous quality control, did it elegantly. The site admins kept Oink organized. BitTorrent architecture kept Oink efficient.

Oink was shuttered in 2007, only months after I first logged on. Too late. Oink's alleged 180,000 users didn't forget how useful it was. A handful of sites based on the same concept sprang up in the months after Oink closed. It was common to see users with the Oink pig avatar on all of them. Oink didn't die. It simply became sturdier, more multiple. When Napster croaked back in 2001, a lot of people wondered how they'd ever access all that music again.

Unauthorized file-sharing is so much easier now—and less necessary with the rise of streaming. The overall movement is toward *more* ways to share music and ideas with like-minded individuals on the Internet. The way I see it, this can only be a good thing for music fans. And what musician is not first a music fan?

One thing bugs me about Oink and its children: the priggism of only allowing commercial releases. It didn't cost money to use Oink, yet the site only accepted official retail releases. The replacement sites followed suit. If you're gonna let individuals share sound with a minimum of centralized interference, why bother to follow the logic of commercial markets? The Shatila collection wouldn't make the cut. All those DJ mixtapes I collected in the nineties? Nope. I have hundreds of MP3 CDs purchased in street markets all over the globe; I'd get kicked off if I tried to share them in the post-Oink sites. They lost an opportunity to explore how music could spread completely unattached from money, which would be a world away from the role of pirates "liberating" for-sale music.

How to hold on? What we care for we repeat.

MUSICALIZE MONEY

Music is a fluid, so wherever it comes to a stop, you'll find a lot of forces at work. For Said and the Palestinians, these forces are about memory and cultural self-determination. For the Oinkers, the motivation to collect cleaves along techno-deterministic lines: we share these files because we can.

As is, the bulk of humanity's audiovisual cultural records lies in the grip of places such as YouTube. Before any platform can stream, it must first warehouse all relevant data. To put it delicately, streaming services are our default music libraries, and they're crap. Strangely, public conversation around streaming boils down to "Hey, can companies make money off this? Look how little they give the artists!" Economic questions elbow their way in front of a cultural debate. Every time I see an article like that, I want to yell out, *"We're inside the infinite library!* Let's start showing a sense of wonder and respect!"

It's always eye-opening to follow the money, but when we let questions of profit displace questions of cultural stewardship, the discussion goes flat. The cornucopia of recorded music constitutes an unthinkably vast array of different types of expression, all of which have something to say about what it is to be human. A lot of weird, unclassifiable stuff is out there, and only a fraction of it is meant to be commercialized. How might we better discuss and facilitate access to such things? And how wide is that *we*? Anybody with Web access can upload to YouTube, but who has the right to remove things from it? Right now, only a tiny sliver of interested parties can delete records contained in the Universal Jukebox. Corporate containers can't hold the Infinite Library and shouldn't try to.

The Wu-Tang Clan and I don't see eye to eye on this.

I was one of about a hundred people who attended what was billed as the first and last listening session for the Staten Island rap collective's final album, *Once Upon a Time in Shaolin.* Their idea, as explained by the group's leader, producer RZA, was to make a unique artwork. Like the *Mona Lisa*, he said. The sole copy of the album, we were told, is a double CD held in the vault of a Marrakech luxury hotel, to be auctioned off to a single buyer. The whole thing struck me as silly, but the invitation promised a listen, and I couldn't pass that up. What happened serves as a cautionary tale about the ridiculousness of artificial scarcity in the twenty-first century.

The party was held at the Museum of Modern Art's PS1 space in Queens on one of those bitterly cold winter nights when the snow, now rat-colored with grime, has hardened into ice and the wind blows in your face no matter which direction you're walking. Several dozen of us showed up on time, but even so we had to wait outside for nearly half an hour for no apparent reason. Then security began letting people in five at a time. Making people queue outside an empty club is the original artificial scarcity.

Once inside, we were subjected to airport-grade security theater, with patdowns, metal detectors, and the taking away of all electronic devices. After I made it through all that, I assumed there'd be at least free drinks or Cheez-It crackers. But no. The space had a hundred or so chairs set up, each with a bottle of water on it. Prepping us, in a way, for the marathon wait to come. A classical concerto played on the speakers. The handcrafted Moroccan nickel silver box that didn't contain the CDs (or silver for that matter—nickel silver is brass) lay on a pedestal, surrounded by little velvet ropes. On either side, a security guard and/or male model dressed as a security guard stood sternly eyeing the audience. We had nothing to look at except the box and a slide show above the box depicting photos of the box.

After forty-five minutes, a PS1 curator welcomed us, then handed the mic to the Paddle8 auctioneer, who shouted plati-

tudes about art and value at us before ceding it to RZA and his
Moroccan megafan Tarik "Cilvaringz" Azzougarh, who actually
produced the album. The men told us how they were riding horses
by the Great Pyramids in Egypt and decided to make something
for the ages. Comparisons to *Mona Lisa*, Picasso, etc., etc.

Then they played thirteen minutes of the two-hour-plus
album. Those thirteen minutes contained five excerpted songs
interspersed with what appeared to be ads for their project. All
of the songs were bad—no, not bad. Merely dated and shapeless
early-nineties Wu boom bap, without any creative sampling.
The final song had a soul horn sample built into it and could
actually have gotten radio play back in 1995, if only they'd
turned up Method Man's brief verse in the mix.

Then a journalist joined the two onstage and launched one
softball question after another. Questions so insubstantial they
evaporated on contact. I mean, it's actively interesting (by *interesting* I mean corny as hell) that RZA decided to make an
album for one member of the 1 percent. Why not at least broach
that topic? Does enforced artificial scarcity work without big
spenders keeping things exclusive? It's an actual question, one
that someone might have asked in some form had there been an
audience Q&A. But there was none.

I scurried out into the night.

The elephant in the room is that RZA probably tried to sell
the album to a major label, but Wu-Tang's lack of a substantial
album-buying fan base, combined with the stuck-in-a-time-
capsule music on it, meant that nobody was biting. Their previous

record sold sixty thousand copies. It's a respectable number in today's consumer climate, but RZA was right in betting that a single sale would pull in more cash. His move was at once ridiculous and canny—and apparently done without consulting the Clan's other members.

The Giza Pyramids inspiration story struck me as particularly apt: stunts such as these entomb the music. For the record, Wu-Tang rapper and actor Method Man agrees with me. *XXL* reported his reaction to learning details of the one-off album stunt as "When music can't be music and y'all turning it into something else, f—— that. Give it to the people. If they want to hear the shit, let them have it. Give it away free. I don't give a f——; that ain't making nobody rich or poor. Give the f——ing music out. Stop playing with the public, man."

Eight months later Paddle8 auction house announced *Once Upon a Time in Shaolin*'s sale to an anonymous buyer, for an undisclosed sum. A few weeks after that it was revealed that Paddle8 had delayed naming the buyer because of his notoriety. They'd previously sold Kurt Cobain's Visa card to the man in question, Martin Shkreli. Weeks before the *Shaolin* reveal, the finance executive hit international headlines when he suddenly hiked up the price of a critical anti-infection drug more than 5,500 percent. The decision had the greatest impact on those with weakened immune systems: HIV and cancer patients, pregnant mothers, and very young children. The drug is no longer patented, but Shkreli created a closed distribution network that made it unfeasible for any competition to access the drug in hopes of developing a generic version for less. Big Pharma is the ultimate in enforced artificial scarcity.

"You know," Shkreli confided to *Bloomberg*, referring to RZA and rapper Fetty Wap in particular or black entertainers in general, "at the right price these guys basically will do anything." A few days after the Wu-Tang announcement, Shkreli unveiled a plan to jack up the price of an antiparasite drug treatment used primarily by poor immigrants from South America—who could previously access it for free.

Imagine an economy based on music. Value would be widespread, contagious even. Impossible not to share. After all, music fosters exchange while being suspicious of authority and ownership. How do you measure a song? Three minutes (time), four megabytes (space), $1 to own, or 0.00012 cents per stream (money, barely). The best measurements can't be quantified. When one song takes root in the countless people who memorize it. When a chorus lifts a roomful of strangers up into a shared emotion. The sound track to a first kiss that's able to stop lovers in their tracks decades later. The value of those songs lies in us.

Monetizing music isn't half as fun as musicalizing money. What would that look like—full communism or even weirder? *Give the ~~music~~ money out. Stop playing with the public.*

Your guess is as good as mine.

This I know: a truly meaningful musical event can happen at any scale. One is moved by a sound, a scene, a two-note riff. More important than the form is how it exacts its magic on us—popular songs such as the *dabke* that Tame passed me voice their times in a way that everyone understands intuitively: a summer jam literally enlivens the air for a season. Some artists send shock waves forward, influencing contemporaries and swaying trends. Others reach back to reconfigure how we hear and understand music made years before. A great song becomes a memory palace with room for everybody inside.

10

ACTIVE LISTENING

Swan, the protagonist of Kim Stanley Robinson's novel *2312*, spliced bird genes into her system so that she could whistle really, really well. In Ann Leckie's *Ancillary Justice*, the main character is a military artificial intelligence whose favorite pastime is taking over the bodies of soldiers it has captured and strolling the city it now occupies with them, making their vocal cords sing old Americana songs in chorus with itself. "The Hydrogen Sonata" is an irredeemably bad piece of music in Iain M. Banks's novel of the same name. It gained notoriety for being universally unappealing yet difficult to perform— humans must graft an extra pair of arms onto their body to play it. John Brunner's *Stand on Zanzibar* predicts a future (set in 2010!) where polyrhythms are yesterday's news: full-on arrhythmic clashing dominates the pop charts.

Sounds of the future. Who's taking bets? As for me, I leave those extrapolations to the sci-fi writers and get nervous when app developers or industry cats say they've found answers.

The future always arrives a bit late. Listening to a song I love, I don't want it to end. Music needs time to unfold, as sure as that unfolding directs our attention to the mysterious moment of now. The line "my presence is a present" appears in rap lyrics throughout the years. As a statement of ego, it's not so hot: rooms generally rearrange themselves to become less interesting when famous rappers walk into them. So I started listening against the intended meaning. *This nowness I inhabit is a gift.* There, that's better. How to make the most of it? Good music suggests that every moment is provisional. The details matter more than the scale.

MUSIC FROM SAHARAN CELL PHONES

Christopher Kirkley was living in Brooklyn when a roommate passed him the desert blues music of guitarist Afel Bocoum. "It really drew me in," he told me over coffee. "It was a guitar album, and I couldn't wrap my head around it. There are a lot of polyrhythms in Malian guitar playing, and I couldn't figure out what tunings they were using or how they were doing it. At the same time, I'd decided to leave New York and embark on a recording trip. I'd been listening to a lot of American folk music. You listen to these old songs and can hear what's happening in the background. There's this great recording of farmworkers in Fresno and a train goes by as this woman's singing. I was really intrigued by those aspects of preservation and recording and archiving. That synced up with hearing this beautiful guitar music from Mali." Kirkley ended up spending two years there. He journeyed overland from Morocco, living like a local to absorb the culture and stretch his wallet. He spent a season in Mauritania learning French, fell into work as a wedding recordist, took a detour into Senegal, and finally ended up in the desert outpost city of Kidal, Mali. Along the way Kirkley got really good at playing Enrique Iglesias's "Hero." When he showed up in a small village, guitar in hand, that was what folks most wanted to hear him play, although Chris Brown requests came close.

The experience could have ended there—a long vacation living on the cheap in rural Africa. Instead, upon returning to his hometown of Portland, Oregon, Kirkley started a blog, *Sahelsounds*, to share the field recordings he'd made. His posts dedicated as much attention to the wider context of music-making in the region as to the tunes themselves, in welcome contrast to blogs that breathlessly post little-known music with zero interest in learning more about where it came from.

In the Sahel, Kirkley saw desert vistas of unparalleled beauty. To glimpse the musical landscape, however, he discovered no better place to look than on people's cell phones. Specifically, by trading songs via the memory cards of cell phones in Mali, which Kirkley did for months. They contained Tuareg electric-guitar wedding music and Dire Straits, Bollywood-influenced Nigerian rap and German techno-pop. He upped a ZIP of his favorite selections to *Sahelsounds*, describing it as "music that is immensely popular on the unofficial mp3/cellphone network from Abidjan to Bamako to Algiers, but has limited or no commercial release."

The handful of cassette copies he dubbed back in Portland were quickly snapped up. Interest spread. The backstory of lo-fi, hi-speed off-line digital distribution made for a great press hook. *Music from Saharan Cellphones* playfully challenged dusty stereotypes of the isolated Saharan desert with proof of just how far connectivity has spread—and just how tapped into global production trends music from an African backwater can be.

Sahelsounds soon evolved into a record label and long-term production platform (coordinating tours, events, exhibitions) that points toward how we can all take advantage of this strange twenty-first-century digital sprawl to support meaningful work. What started as a ZIP-file compilation led to a crowd-funded vinyl series, and Kirkley slingshot the attention into yet more ambitious projects. He specializes in vinyl LPs with well-researched liner notes aimed at a Western connoisseur market. To keep the sounds moving, he offers lots of free downloads too. Kirkley helps various groups gain entrée into the international touring circuit, with the stated goal of giving them enough assistance to be able to navigate the world of booking agents and tour offers on their own. He's not trying to maintain a middleman position: it's a success when Sahel Sounds artists can make their own way.

For his Western audience, Kirkley applies centrifugal force that nudges us away from the center. We're encouraged to listen farther afield, to linger with a place and its sounds as Kirkley has done.

For the musicians from in and around Mali that he works with, Sahel Sounds acts as a conduit bringing them closer to the power lines of globalized cool. He helps various global-South musicians to attain visibility in the West *and* have a say in the narratives that form around them. Allowing this awareness of imbalances in access and power to shape how, and for whom, the Sahel Sounds project operates is what I find so compelling. Blog as record label as interface as translation machine. Against the Internet's tendency toward attention-deficit clickbait, YouTube voyeurism, and genre-of-the-week shallowness, Sahel Sounds broadcasts hope for how the Web's connective power can still tap into its utopian promise as a tool to create, then strengthen, alternative networks.

In 2015 Kirkley directed *Rain the Color of Blue with a Little Red in It*. It's the first ever Tashelhit-language fiction film, and it doubles as an homage to Prince's *Purple Rain*. (Tashelhit has no word for "purple.") *Rain* took advantage of the Prince angle to net media coverage and convince on-the-fence viewers to check it out in the Western markets where Sahel Sounds moves. Once they get to the actual movie, they're treated to an understated portrait of life in these desert towns. Indeed, the *Purple*

Rain narrative of music and betrayal nearly gets in the way since the film shines in its unassuming moments—a woman talks of the sea while the camera pans across wavelike desert dunes, some guys make tea in a tent. For those who have not been there, these flashes into the everyday vistas of Sahelian towns and how music activates them are enormous.

The film also serves as a ninety-minute ad for its lead, singer-songwriter Mdou Moctar, whose European and North American tour was timed to coincide with its release. And why not? The closer we get to the Sahel, the less exotic the music becomes, the more entrances we have into it. Sahel Sounds doesn't have the budget to hold publicists on retainer the way bigger labels do; smart moves such as this one help it gain traction.

Despite the intensity and passion with which the electric guitar was taken up in the region, musicians in the Sahel generally don't know Prince, or Jimi Hendrix (despite how bands such as Tinariwen are marketed). They know and love the Scorpions. (I hope Kirkley will release a volume of *Music from Saharan Cellphones* dedicated exclusively to the Western guitar bands that enjoy such popularity in the region.) So as the movie leaps from hard drive to DVD back in Africa, it introduces the exotic music of Prince (and the Revolution) over there.

Sahel Sounds reflects something that has resonated with me throughout my career, what novelist Zora Neale Hurston summarized as *Yuh got tuh go there tuh know there*.

Her phrase isn't about traveling per se. It's a recognition that one's worldview is only that, a single person's outlook, and that so much of life is experiential. If you can't go there, then you'll need to keep quiet and humble and listen to learn what you can from those who have. The guesstimate is always trumped by the reality, and the reality is always messier than our varied descriptions of it.

Go there tuh know there acknowledges that growth happens when we abandon our comfort zones. It means learning the other person's language (musical, cultural, or actual) rather than expecting the person to speak yours. If you feel out of place, then hang around until the feeling ebbs. For Kirkley, this translated to stopping in Mauritania and not leaving until he'd absorbed enough French to hold substantial conversations, with melodious African-accented slang and all, which often causes surprises for people who speak with him on the phone before meeting him in person. *You're white!?* It's great. Language can be a bridge. The small gesture of not defaulting to English (or *French* French) speaks volumes.

Then there is the beauty of small numbers. Of falling into uncrowded corners, seeing the value there, figuring out how to share it without ripping out the heart. Despite all the challenges to a nineties-era do-it-yourself approach, one person can still make a difference while operating at a scale that an established indie label would scoff at as negligible. Put out a thousand-run LP of Tuareg wedding music recorded live on cell phones to be sold to people who have never been to any such wedding? Why not! A small scale allows for greater control over each creation—and obscure music releases demand this care.

While I'm usually happy to see bloated label infrastructures shrivel up, I'm thrilled when like-minded individuals join forces in smaller economic spaces to bring quieter, harder-to-spot scenes to greater attention. Often basic organization makes the difference between being able to tour and earn money from one's music and not, between artists' being taken advantage of by sloppy labels and establishing their own.

That Tuareg wedding LP—it's Sahel Sounds' most recent release, by Timbuktu musician Abba Gargando. "When he starts playing," explains Kirkley, his audience will "switch on their phones, start recording, and throw them onto the floor. It may be simplistic to think we can cut through decades of misappropriation with technology. But it does suggest the increasing role that artists may have in their creation and representation abroad—the Western mediators saying less, because it's already being said."

My favorite story about Kirkley puts him in the spotlight. He was walking in Mali's capital city of Bamako when a group of teens approached him. They'd recognized Kirkley from a cellphone video of him playing on a corner in Timbuktu the week before, more than six hundred miles away. Whoever filmed the clip had shared it with enough friends that it had reached the truckers, who often haul that week's crop of casual data along with their physical goods. The silly fun of seeing a white guy playing guitar in the Malian style traveled over land and on down to these kids. *Gringos on Saharan Cellphones.*

The tools are widespread. We're all looking around, bewildered and delighted. When I think of how difficult it can be to maintain that sense of delight over time, I remember the Ex.

SATISFACTION AND SAXOPHONE REPAIR

The band formed in Amsterdam in 1979. They haven't stopped since. I met them in the early 2000s, when their music was, as a mutual friend put it, "moving more and more in a bizarre but amazing African direction."

Most bands stop innovating after a certain point in their careers (if they ever did), content to rest on their laurels and replicate their past successes. The Rolling Stones' concert audiences tolerate their newer material (songs they wrote anytime during the last thirty years, say) only because of the understanding that they will eventually play "Satisfaction" and other middle-aged hits. I imagine that the Stones' legendary debauchery results from zealous self-medication intended to blunt the existential ennui of life as their own cover band.

With the Ex it is different. Their curiosity and openness work as a kind of perpetual motion machine. They're neither tourists nor tourist attractions. Every few years the band develops a completely new live set, and they're constantly branching out to collaborate with artists from other musical fields.

In 1996, guitarist Terrie Hessels and his family bought a van and spent a year in Africa. Ethiopia blew his mind. The music, the sense of pride in never being colonized, and above all the contagious sharp humor of the place struck a chord for him. He convinced the rest of the band that they needed to visit. And so it began.

The Ethiopia visit became a DIY tour. Pull up in a town with a van and a gas-powered generator, find the police chief to secure permission, then drive around announcing the upcoming concert on a loudspeaker. Thousands would gather to watch these strange and spirited Europeans. The Ex performed arrangements of their favorite Ethiopian songs, often with drummer/vocalist Katherina Bornefeld singing in phonetic Amharic—she became an unlikely star. Occasionally audience members would ask, Why are you here? We have our own music.

Perhaps the best answer to that question came in 2009, when the Ex brought a Dutch horn repairman to Ethiopia with them, his suitcase filled with brass knickknacks. The Ethiopian jazz scene of the sixties and seventies is reasonably well-known due to the French-compiled *Éthiopiques* CD series. Since those golden years it has become increasingly difficult to get spare parts for those aging saxophones and trumpets. The Ex transformed the repairman's hotel room into a service center, and once the word got out, a line of musicians formed up and down the hall. For days.

On the flip side, the Ex invested considerable effort in bringing several of the groups they met to tour with them in Europe. (I joined them on a number of tours, which put me in the rare position of having heard more Ethiopian music performed live than on record.) Their efforts strengthen the artistic paths of everyone they come across. This is what I find so striking about how they exist as a band: they take immense care to ensure that their friends and collaborators weave together to create the strongest network possible. This is achieved in the most straightforward of ways: by being up-front about money and

opportunities, then proceeding via belief in the power of musical collaboration in which all members have an equal say and
investment in the sounds created. After that, the other details
tend to fall into place.

To be clear, I don't trust people who say, "We're living in times
of incredible upheaval; make your own rules, blaze your own
path." Those people probably have a safety net. Maybe it's family
money, rental income, behind-the-scenes social connections,
something. Fact is, while the main beast of the music industry
is indeed in a crazed scrabbling—lobsters realizing that the pot
of water has started to boil—certain rarely spoken yet powerful
rules are extremely difficult to bend. The music biz loves youth.
Sex sells. Controversy sells. Making quality music—whatever *that*
is—has no direct bearing on one's popularity. Pretty is way easier
to sell than ugly. Same goes for skinny. As mixed up as our listening habits and actual lives become, many genres remain heavily
coded by class and ethnic identification. I'm not saying follow
the rules—that would be weird—but I do urge an awareness of
them, if only to depart from them with a reasonable expectation of what challenges one will face. The Ex's no-nonsense
approach is refreshing precisely for facing the difficulties of
making a living from strange music head-on.

Whatever the future is, it starts with us. One doesn't have to
travel to another country or learn saxophone repair to help create a better world for music and those who love it.

My friend Andy Moor from the Ex said to me, "You know
when you're trying to sleep on someone's kitchen floor and the

refrigerator hum is really loud?" I laughed. Because this sort of thing, to a certain type of musician, is common. You start in the dirt. That's where things grow. You stay humble. The sound carries you. If you've done enough DIY touring, at some point the living room is filled up, the bedrooms are all occupied, and someone has to crash in the kitchen. That's how it is.

Early on in my career a cash-strapped Irish promoter invited me to DJ in Dublin. The guy seemed to get what I was doing and promised a good time. Discussing what he could offer, I told him that I was cool crashing on a sofa if that meant I could pocket the money he'd spend on a hotel. This made the difference between getting paid zero and getting €75. I said yes. *Stay hungry*, I thought. *Because you're not gonna start at the top.* And there's no shame in starting at the bottom. That's where most artists worth their salt begin. As long as each step is raising you up, it's all good.

It was my first time in Ireland. As I taxied from the airport to the club (I'd arrived midevening, just a few hours before my set), a U2 song came on the radio. My driver started singing along. It was cute. Then the song ended and the station played another, different U2 song. My taxi driver kept singing the first one. It was amazing. Right then and there I decided that I loved Ireland. That affable, loopy vibe continued into, and after, my gig.

The promoter hadn't mentioned that an afterparty was planned for his living room, and by extension, the couch where I was supposed to sleep. I discovered this as I was preparing for bed once we'd returned. I had an early-morning flight. Then friends, DJs, buddies, came over. Somehow everyone had eaten magic mushrooms except me. Not that I would have taken them—post-9/11 airport security for a young black man traveling alone is complicated enough (just because you're paranoid doesn't mean you're not being unconstitutionally stopped and searched) without piling on the effects of ingesting contraband hallucinogenic fungus. So that was the scene: €75, frozen pizza for dinner, and a woman DJing in the kitchen, decks set up over the sink. (How can you not love the Irish?) When the afterparty stumbled out toward an after-afterparty, I caught a few hours of sleep on that couch.

It was a good weekend. I believed in what I was doing, and I believed in the networks of fellow artists and committed supporters and strange wild stuff I'd see along the way. The promoter cleaned up his act, and while we never worked together again, I was back in Dublin before long, with a decent fee and a hotel room and an equally shambolic club night.

Some people are good at getting and keeping jobs. I'm not one of them. I've never had a safety net, a day job, or a trust fund to siphon off of. This is the polite way of saying I've been close to broke on many occasions, but miraculously, managed to stay on the right side of things. By living frugally. By working as much as possible. For example, for years I'd make a CD-R mixtape before each tour. Burn up a hundred copies at the Harlem Xerox spots, stash 'em in my luggage, sell for five bucks a pop at shows.

I don't believe in the value of hard work in and of itself, and bootstrapping oneself up from a working-class background to comfortable middle class looks increasingly like a thing of the past, at least in America. But artists have always operated in a margin of implausibility. We are necessary even if what we create is necessarily useless.

From a financial perspective, music is sheer nonsense. Even at the plush record labels, a handful of bestselling artists subsidize the operations of everybody else. Before the nineties the figure was 10 percent. I'm guessing that it'll grow even smaller. One "Gangnam Style" equals one hundred thousand other Korean pop songs. To me this is license to keep listening further afield, to chase the sound around the corner, to understand that the spotlight follows the money but our ears are free to go elsewhere. It's a call to participate. Understanding what music means and how it moves helps to explain why the world is the way it is.

Musicians shouldn't assume ideal listeners. Rather, we should try to become ideal listeners.

WITH LISTENING COMES RESPONSIBILITY

As someone whose main source of income stems from providing live entertainment in nightclubs, I know full well that folks go there to "party and bullshit," as the Notorious B.I.G. rapped. But there's room for social realism in the club too. Despite occasional typos on my concert flyers in Asian countries, I am *not* DJ Rapture. My job may facilitate drunken celebration, but nobody's telling me what to play or how to play it. I don't have to ecstatically pump my fists as I play one you-must-have-fun dance-floor track after another. Crowds love DJs who do this, but I'm proof that you can sneak unorthodox musical selections past the bouncers. (Proceed with caution if you choose this path: my booking agency did dump me last year.)

For a while I would end club DJ sets with a turntablist routine involving one of my favorite Tracy Chapman songs. After whipping the dance floor into a frenzy, I'd let the final beat die out, then stop the record with the needle still placed directly on the vinyl. The trick creates an ultralow, stomach-churning hum. Bass feedback sounds like a mistake. The forceful constant tone it generates will often cause bits of the room itself to shake, so you get such things as loose AC units buzzing in resonance, adding to the ominous effect. Sometimes I'd tap out a rhythm on the stopped record—the technique makes the turntable into an amplified drumhead.

When you kill a beat, people keep dancing for a few moments in hopes that you'll bring it back. When they realize it's not coming back, you get a roomful of sweaty people, staring, waiting to see what's next. Drunks will shout; you hope it's praise. When that moment hit, I'd slip in Chapman's chilling "Behind the Wall" on top of the low-end feedback. "Last night I heard the screaming, loud voices behind the wall," she begins, using just enough melody to let us know that she's singing instead of speaking. It's a great way to end a party! Seriously. A DJ set is about the creation of communal momentum, so switching that up at the end can make for a powerful conclusion.

And besides, Tracy Chapman's "Behind the Wall" is the best parable of listening that I know of. First off, it's a cappella:

there is only her voice to hold on to (a cappellas are catnip for DJs since they can be mixed with other records so easily). Solo performances usually showcase the singer's vocal chops. Here Chapman's androgynous voice sounds strong yet exhausted, too tired for adornment, almost defenseless as it directs attention to her words. "Behind the Wall" narrates the harrowing tale of a woman who hears, bleeding through the walls of her apartment, the sound of another woman being beaten by her husband. Hearing the abuse night after night has made the listener a witness. Witnessing the injustice without acting on it has, in some small way, made her an accomplice. She's moved yet doesn't know how to help.

The narrator considers calling the police yet knows they will neither arrive in time nor be able to help with these "domestic affairs." There's none of the easy anti-cop talk common in hip-hop. For all their authority, the cops are outside the situation, whereas the simple fact of living within earshot links the listener to this couple's violent intimacies, and to the possibility of helping. Sound is what unites their domestic space with hers, and this unity demarcates community. But what is to be done?

The penultimate stanza of "Behind the Wall" tells of a night when the screaming ends in a terrible silence. An ambulance comes, a crowd gathers, the cops tell them to "disperse"—go home, dissolve the power of the crowd. Locking the door behind you in your own home does not ensure safety, nor does it keep out sound.

The scene could offer a conclusion, but the song and the situation it describes doesn't end there. The final stanza repeats the first. Chapman's song structure mirrors the cycle of violence she describes, and this lack of a conclusion is part of the point. "Behind the Wall" ends where it begins, with a great deal of pain and no catharsis in sight.

The thing that crosses the line between public and private is sound itself. Sound permeates walls, turning everyone's interior space a bit more public. Listening connects the woman alone in her apartment with the social world outside it. If you can hear it, it's happening right now. Nearby and in time for you to take action. Sound creates community even, perhaps especially, when we don't want it. This is the great lesson of "Behind the Wall": with listening comes responsibility.

After each performance, someone would invariably approach me saying, "Great set, Rupture, but why did you have to play that last song? That was such a downer!" I did it to remind people—myself first and foremost—that DJing doesn't have to always kowtow to the pleasure principle, and that there's a world outside the club.

ACKNOWLEDGMENTS

It takes a village to sack a library. If it weren't for all that time spent in libraries as a kid (and adult), this book wouldn't exist, so I say: support your local public library.

So many people were incredibly generous with their time throughout this process. *Gracias merci shukran tenemert* to everyone I interviewed, especially those whose contributions didn't make it into the book.

Parts of *Uproot* previously appeared, in a different form, in articles for *n+1*, *The Fader*, *Frieze*, and *The National*—thanks to editors Peter C. Baker, Dan Fox, Mark Greif, Julianne Escobedo Shepherd, Matthew Schnipper, and Michael Vazquez.

Rocío Salceda, Edward Orloff, and Sean McDonald gifted me with their vision from the beginning. Insight from early readers Anne Boyer, Jess Atwood Gibson, research assistant Aaron Gonsher, Maggie Schmitt, and Schnipper made this a better book. Susu Attar, Yasmin El-Rifae, Maggie Schmitt, Hassan Wargui, and Amy Zhang all provided translation assistance. Contagious positivity from Ruby Lerner, Lisa Dent, and the entire Creative Capital crew helped keep things afloat. The USC Annenberg/Getty Arts Journalism Fellowship brought me to L.A. for a welcome spell. Thanks to my parents, especially for facilitating a DIY residency in Virginia.

Ongoing conversations with Chief Boima, Carlos Delclós, Brad Fox, Geraldine Juárez, Josh Kun, Wayne Marshall, Sonido Martines, Alex Mar, Geoff Manaugh, Andy Moor, Ghislain Poirier, Toy Selectah, Matt Shadetek, and countless others were invaluable.

The FSG team is fantastic; special thanks to Nora Barlow for keeping everything on track, Devin Washburn for the pitch-perfect cover, and Stephen Weil for steering it into the world.

No surrender, no delete!

For endnotes, audio/video clips of the music referenced in Uproot, *and links to explore further, visit uprootbook.com.*